S0-BYC-357

Where the Road Ends

Stories and images from the heart of Crested Butte

Dusty Demerson

Nathan Bilow

Where the Road Ends

Stories and images from the heart of Crested Butte

A collaboration
by Sandy Fails and MJ Vosburg

Photography by
Nathan Bilow, Dusty Demerson, Paul Gallaher,
Chris Ladoulis, J.C. Leacock, Janette Runge,
James Ray Spahn and Tom Stillo

Riverbend Books, LLC
Crested Butte, Colorado

Text by Sandy Fails
Produced by MJ Vosburg
Graphic design by Jessy Moreland, Crested Butte Printing, Inc.
Printed by Crested Butte Printing, Inc.

Cover photo by Janette Runge: Zach Vosburg gazes east toward
Mount Crested Butte from the flanks of Belleview Mountain.

Title page photo by Nathan Bilow:
Gravity + new snow + a day off = one very good morning for skier Kyle Sul.

Contents page photo by Nathan Bilow: Moonrise over the
mountain lends downtown Crested Butte a touch of mystery.

ISBN: 0-615-12986-2

Published and distributed by
Riverbend Books, LLC
P.O. Box 911
Crested Butte, Colorado 81224
www.wheretheroadends.com

Copyright ©2005 by Riverbend Books, LLC.
All rights reserved. No part of this book may be reproduced in any form, except for
brief reviews, without written permission from the publisher.

JC Leacock

Nathan Bilow

Table of Contents

▲ World-class adventure racers Jari Kirkland and Jon Brown are either having fun or training…or having fun training. Photo: Stillo

▶▶ Penstemmon aglow on a cloudy day. Photo: Runge

Preface

This book was born from a friendship, which, happily, survived the rigorous birth. Since this is, among other things, a book of stories, let's start with the tale of that friendship.

Though MJ Vosburg and I arrived in Crested Butte the same year (1981) and married our sweethearts the same year (1982), we knew each other only distantly until we had our sons (yes, the same year — 1987). Then MJ asked if I wanted to take care of her baby a few days a week. I knew her by reputation as a go-getter marketing whiz; she thought of me as a laid-back writer and semi-stay-at-home mom. MJ lived and worked in what I considered the newer, more business-oriented world of Mt. Crested Butte. I lived and worked for the newspaper mostly in old Crested Butte. We seemingly had little in common except our new babies, which was, of course, enormous in those early days of motherhood.

Our first conversations centered around MJ's baby Zach: what he ate, did, produced and said (our boys were both precocious talkers) during my days with him. Zach and my son Chris learned to toddle, jabber and play army together. More slowly, MJ and I learned to jabber and play together, too, until, without planning it, we turned into good friends.

Our boys grew up like cousins. I felt honored to be the godmother of MJ's second child, Emma, and on her special day I passed on to her a bracelet that had belonged to my mom. When my mother and father had died two years earlier, MJ had flown down to Fort Worth twice within a month for their funerals.

In the last two decades, MJ and I have walked untold miles together, taken family vacations together and become confidants, cheerleaders and helpmates. We've driven each other crazy (the go-getter and the laid-back) and taught each other the separate parts of the Serenity Prayer: MJ specializes in "the courage to change the things I can"; I'm better at "the serenity to accept the things I can't"; and over a long-enough lunch we can generally muster "the wisdom to know the difference." MJ also taught me the value of relationships — friends, family, community — which she pursues and honors as loyally as anyone I know.

A few years ago, MJ and I became work associates when she took over ad sales for the *Crested Butte Magazine*, which I had edited since 1986. From that vantage point, we gained new respect for each other's talents.

I write; MJ gets things done. I should have known what would happen when I mentioned the idea of creating a book about Crested Butte. Many people have discussed such a project in the last decade, but MJ jumped from chitchat to business plan without missing a beat.

Our goal was to have fun doing a project together (perhaps partly to distract me from the separation anxiety of sending Chris off to college this fall) and to capture through words and photos the wonder of our home.

Crested Butte has been the backdrop to our lives and the lives of our children. It has been both the topic and the setting for hikes with our dogs (the barker and the shedder), cross-country ski outings and family dinners around the Vosburg table with its classic views of Paradise Divide.

MJ and I probably wouldn't have become friends, surrogate sisters or work associates had we lived in a larger, more stratified community. And, as she put it, we would never have had the guts to publish a book about a place that wasn't small and intimate enough that we could wrap our arms around it.

Many other people loaned their talents to this book. Our thanks to the photographers who contributed images of such beauty, character and humor, and to the people we interviewed for letting us use their stories as a glance into the heart of Crested Butte. Our gratitude to Jessy Moreland, Steve Mabry and the gang at Crested Butte Printing for transforming our ingredients into a book; to our husbands, Michael and Joel, and kids for their support during the process; and to our friends for sanity breaks along the way.

We created this book for all who share the bond of Crested Butte, whether this is their home, the home of their hearts, or a discovery they're about to make. May this book remind us that, if Crested Butte is part of our lives, we have one big blessing in common.

—Sandy Fails

▲ On hushed, misty mornings, Elk Avenue's old buildings keep their secrets to themselves. Photo: Spahn

▲ Against an imposing mountain backdrop, Crested Butte's closely clustered neighborhoods feel even more intimate.

The BIG Picture

❧

This road to the heart of the mountains

Nathan Bilow

▲ Nature's grand artistry: A Beckwith Mountain vista in mid September. Photo: Leacock

▶▶ Beauty in the details: Frosty morning etching on an autumn leaf. Photo: Runge

Getting closer

Never mind objectivity. This book gazes at Crested Butte from the least objective viewpoint possible: through the eyes of people who love it. The words in this book came from conversations on hikes, on chairlifts and around kitchen tables. How better to capture Crested Butte than through its stories?

First let's set the stage for those stories. Watching "The Sound of Music" for the tenth time recently, I noted that, even with hearts to be broken and Nazis to escape, the filmmakers took time to swoop over the mountains, lakes and villages of Austria before settling onto the hillside where Julie Andrews waited to burst into song. Hey, if it worked for "The Sound of Music"….

Let's start rolling our imaginary aerial camera about 10,000 feet above the ground, soaring north from Gunnison so Highway 135 traces a gray thread through the rich greens of the valley floor. Those black specks are cows, fat and happy in bovine nirvana. Around them, verdant meadows laced with snowmelt-heavy streams sweep gradually upward to the north, with isolated, white-capped peaks — Round Mountain, Whetstone, Crested Butte — jutting abruptly from the green expanse. Following the gray thread northward, our view ends with a formidable range of mountains, a gleaming white mass wrapping north, east and west, giving the sense that here ends the accessible world.

Gliding up the valley toward these massive peaks, the camera descends a little lower over the town of Crested Butte, a few square blocks of tidy, colorful homes nestled neighborly in the valley floor. Intriguing... we'll be back.

First let's follow the highway, now a mellow two-lane road, as it meanders three miles up the hillside to a community of larger, modern buildings: the town of Mt. Crested Butte. Oddly, this last outpost of civilization before the alpine wilderness is also the most contemporary in the county. Cranes and crews at the town's center bear witness to the new ski resort rising from the old. From this base area, chairlifts climb the broad ski mountain, with its jagged spires to the south, friendly rolls to the west and unruly steeps to the north.

At the north end of Mt. Crested Butte, our road turns to dirt, then disappears beneath the snowbanks still lingering from late winter's heavy storms. Beyond, we see no further signs of civilization, just towering mountains with stretches of rock and earth starting to show through their snowy mantles.

As our camera banks a turn back toward Crested Butte, we drop lower still. A few narrow dirt roads spoke outward from Crested Butte into the drainages between the peaks; this early in spring, all eventually fade beneath high-country snow. Most of these roads were forged first by prospectors more than a century ago as dreams of gold lured them ever farther into the wilds. Occasional black-gray tailings piles or log cabin ruins below us give the only other hint of the mining camps and boomtowns that sprouted and collapsed in this rugged country.

Still circling back toward town, we spy hikers hauling their skis up Mt. Emmons for a morning of classic spring skiing. The snowfields they seek feed the icy cascades plunging down Oh-Be-Joyful Creek, where whitewater-hungry kayakers scout harrowing routes. A mile downstream, where the creek joins the Slate River, three kids, still wearing light jackets in the coolness, throw sticks into the water for their retriever pup, while Mom and Dad sip coffee brewed over their morning campfire. A little closer to town, two mountain bikers pause on the Lower Loop to watch a deer graze on the hillside above them.

For a moment we drift east above the Slate River, then turn toward Crested Butte, glancing at the cemetery where gravestone names like Krizmanich, Tezak and Sporcich hint at the immigrant miners and their families who anchored the community for much of the twentieth century.

Arriving at the edge of town, we follow a woman on a fat-tired townie bike with plastic flowers laced into its oversized basket. She hollers, "Hi, Hon!" and stops to chat with someone in a passing car. The driver in the car behind waits patiently; heaven forbid a Crested Buttean should honk. Oh, our bicyclist is on the move

▲ Local personality Heli Peterson pedals her trademark wheels back from a mid-day ski with her roommate, Jenny. Photo: Stillo

again, turning down Elk Avenue. We skim down the main street of town now, just above the false-fronted Victorians — tall, skinny buildings shoulder to shoulder with other tall, skinny buildings, most with tall, skinny windows. Some brave souls have already planted their window boxes with flowers, though the nights may still be frosty for several weeks. Already this morning, people have settled with their coffee cups on Elk Avenue's benches, some made of old car parts revived as sittable art. Outside the post office, yet another Crested Butte volunteer sells raffle tickets for yet another good cause.

Another turn and we're in a neighborhood of simple old houses — saggy, splintery shacks tucked in between face-lifted dollhouses. Our flying camera pauses at a lace-curtained window. What faces might we see inside?

Maybe we'll see the Ruggeras, now in their eighties: Willard, musician and character-about-town who ran Crested Butte back in its pre-ski days, and Ronnie, who cared for three generations of town kids after raising her own children. Or perhaps painter and theater veteran Patricia Dawson, who came to Crested Butte during the "hippie" era and grew into a local matron of the arts. Perhaps we'll tap on the window of Alison Gannett's strawbale house to visit the extreme skier, mountaineer and renewable resource activist. Or maybe we'll catch the Hensley family at the breakfast table: Chris, director of the Adaptive Sports Center, and Sally, who taught half the kids in town their ABCs at Stepping Stones Children's Center before mothering her own two sons. Chris and Sally met in Crested Butte shortly after college and launched their careers and family here. Then again, maybe we'll see Ellie Deacon, a spirited Florida retiree who learned to hike, paddle and get her manicured hands dirty with her lady friends in Crested Butte.

All of these folks are part of the mix of Crested Butte, which gains something from each: work ethic and sense of community from its miners; creativity and fun from its hippies and Rastafarians; adventure and play from its outdoor athletes; strength and continuity from its families; culture and amenities from its generous second homeowners. Unlike in more striated towns, all belong to a single community, made more intimate by its smallness, isolation and the domination of the natural landscape around it. And, of course, by its wealth of shared stories.

So, let's put the aerial camera aside and settle in at our figurative kitchen table, to get to know Crested Butte through the stories of its people.

▲ Dwarf mutant columbine: How many colors can one flower wear? Photo: Runge

▲ From 12,000 feet elevation you can scope out your favorite run *and* your après-ski hot tub. Photo: Bilow

▲ Winter landscapes inspire calm reflection. Photo: Leacock

▼ At the Gothic general store, runners start their Fourth of July with an eight-mile "run, walk or crawl" in the Gothic-Crested Butte One-Third Marathon. Photo: Ladoulis

▶▶ How better to cruise Crested Butte's quaint, snowy neighborhoods than by horse-drawn sleigh? Photo: Ladoulis

▲ Downtown Crested Butte, from the snowbanks up. Photo: Demerson

▲▶ How Lily Lake got its name. Photo: Demerson

▼ What some skiers do when their snow melts into whitewater. Photo: Runge

▼▶ Snow buddies Shannon Holleran and Asya Stillo. Photo: Stillo

▼▶▶ Wheels abandoned in favor of powder boards. Photo: Demerson

▲   At the drop of a hat (or boa), Suzanne Hadley trades her parka for Mardi Gras finery. Photo: Ladoulis

▼   Snow creates a textured canvas for the play of winter light. Photo: Leacock

▶▶ Essential soccer gear: shin-guards, cleats and comfort objects. Photo: Ladoulis

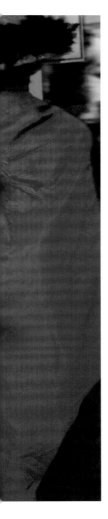

▲ A ghostly moon slides down behind Oh-Be-Joyful.

Beyond the Reach of Roads

❧

The power of Crested Butte's wild spaces

Nathan Bilow

▲   The fading day throws a last wash of color over the East River. Photo: Runge

▶▶ Pastor Tim Clark infuses his ceremonies with plein-air reverence. Photo: Ladoulis

Habitat for the holy

Pastor Tim Clark intertwines his outdoor explorations
with his spiritual ones.

The Reverend Tim Clark looks equally at home in his white liturgical robes
or his sweaty bike shorts — different vestments for the different altars of his life.

The great stretches of wildness around Crested Butte feed Tim's soul as
surely as the golden-lit sanctuary of the Union Congregational Church, where he
has served as pastor since 1992. To Tim, Crested Butte's nearby mountains, canyons
and rivers are not just super-sized playgrounds; they are also "habitat for the holy."

One early-spring day, when patches of snow still dotted the young wildflower fields, Tim was riding his mountain bike alone out Deer Creek when he
caught in his peripheral vision a sense that the forest was "flowing" up the hill. He
stopped his bike and turned to see at least 200 elk, many of them young calves, moving up the flanks of Whiterock Mountain toward their summer territory. After gaz-
ing at them in awe, Tim pedaled ahead up the trail, stashed his bike and crouched
down among the new wildflowers — right in the path of the herd. To his delight,
they meandered closely around him, giving him a rare look — and listen — at elk
social life.

"They moved right through me," he said. "The cows were teaching the
young ones to communicate. They'd call and the calves would squeak and beep and

blurp, trying to learn the language. To me, that is being present at a sacred ceremony. How can that not stir your soul?"

From his Connecticut boyhood, fishing, skiing, hiking and pondering grand philosophical questions lying under the outstretched "arms" of an ancient oak, Tim's outdoor explorations have been interwoven with his spiritual ones. At college in Oregon, he learned to fly fish, rock climb, sand surf and mountaineer while studying world religions and indigenous theologies. At the Union Theological Seminary in New York, he wrote his thesis on experiencing spirit in the outdoors.

Also at the seminary, Tim looked more squarely at humanity's sometimes-forsaken stewardship role, and the relationship between people, nature and spirit became a personal imperative. "Are we fouling our own nest, a nest of sacred origin? I began to think maybe this could be my contribution — to spend more time and energy trying to heal the brokenness that has occurred between humans and nature. To re-examine the archaic view of nature as simply the raw material for progress, to reclaim its sacredness."

In his years as a pastor in Crested Butte, Tim's belief in the power and sacredness of wild places has been continually reinforced, partly through personal experience. His pastoral role requires a strong spiritual connection, but also fills his calendar with everyday human demands. Taking forays into the wilds around Crested Butte not only strengthens his quads and clears his lungs, it also replenishes him in a deeper way. Perhaps that explains how he maintains his trademark blend of glee, mischief, wisdom and reverence.

"I need sanctuary from social interactions. I need quiet, to take time to listen to sounds and smell smells, let all my senses be stimulated. The top of a mountain, floating a river, hiking… that allows me the time and place away from structure, schedule, having to communicate."

That also opens Tim's life to the "little pockets of wonder" he finds everywhere in Crested Butte's backcountry, from hidden cascades and glorious vistas to unexpected wildlife encounters. On a knife-edge ridge out past Oh Be Joyful, he backed away from a standoff with a hoof-stomping mountain goat. Biking out Baxter Gulch, Tim stopped to watch a mother cow chase a full-grown bear across a meadow, a bear so startled by the bovine's bodacious maternal rage that it tucked its rear end down like a scared dog as she rammed it a couple of times from behind.

"I laughed so hard I fell off my bike," Tim said. "It made me appreciate that the Divine sense of humor goes far beyond anything I could conjure up."

As he counsels other individuals, Tim also witnesses nature's power to rejuvenate and change people. "I see it all the time. Sometimes it's as simple as watch-

▲ A bighorn sheep blends into its craggy post near Almont's wildlife reserve. Photo: Runge

■ Geese prepare for take-off from a slippery runway. Photo: Demerson

▼ In the dappled light of an aspen glen, deer and camera exchange a stare. Photo: Bilow

ing a flight of geese and losing track of time and place and self long enough that when you come back, you're not the same any more — and know you never will be. Sometimes nature takes us out of ourselves enough that we can make the changes we've needed to make for a long time."

So many people who live in or visit Crested Butte sense that same power and choose to incorporate the outdoors into their rituals of spirit, from baptisms to weddings to memorials. Yes, that introduces risk; one drenched couple hollered their vows over the pounding fury of a sudden violent hailstorm. But it also throws open the door for unpredictable blessings. Ending a recent wedding above Lake Irwin, Tim proclaimed, "May the mountains break forth in music before you," and the couple turned to start their married life under the celestial awning of a huge double rainbow.

During the quietest moments of outdoor ceremonies, as humans gather still and hushed, wild animals are sometimes drawn by their own curiosity, adding another element of wonder to the ritual. Tim delighted in a buck and doe who gathered close to observe a couple's betrothal in the woods. In a wedding he performed on a dog-sledding outing, an ermine popped unexpectedly out of the snow between the bride and groom, gazed at one and then the other as they exchanged vows, then disappeared just as abruptly as they shared their first kiss as husband and wife. Tim has also had doves, herons and other winged beings grace his ceremonies as though on cue.

Not surprisingly, Tim and his wife Kelley Jo tied the knot outdoors, on a multi-day rafting trip with friends and family. After solemnly sharing their vows on their rock outcropping/wedding altar, they leaped hand in hand into the river below, to the yahoos of their loved ones. The reverence, playfulness and natural setting seemed a fitting start for their married life in Crested Butte, surrounded in all directions by beauty "created by hands larger than our own," Tim said.

"This is one of the most beautiful places I've ever seen," he said of Crested Butte. "And the culture embraces that… so the natural beauty and the ability to engage it and the way people live their lives are totally inseparable. This culture could not exist in another place. And this place could not be appreciated or loved as deeply through any other culture." ✧

▲ From here, all things seem possible. Photo: Spahn

▲   Winter gets a jump on autumn in this Beckwith Mountain landscape. Photo: Leacock

▼   This ptarmigan has traded its winter white for summer's mottled camouflage. Photo: Runge

▶▶ Sneezeweed edges a beaver pond out Kebler Pass Road. Photo: Runge

▲ The Gunsight bridge beneath winter's frozen calm. Photo: Stillo

▲ Snowmelt swells the cascades that tumble down the hillsides outside Crested Butte. Photo: Leacock

▲   Flax adds its hue to the summer micro-landscape. Photo: Runge

▶▶ Flower convert Don Hempel traded his hammer for a hand lens. Photo: Gallaher

Belly flowers

How Crested Butte's wildflowers brought Don Hempel down to earth.

Don Hempel's Crested Butte hiking buddies are hardly surprised when they stop on the trail to check the topo map and turn to find Don crouched among the wildflowers with micro lens in hand, exclaiming about the delicate formations of a bishop's cap or Siberian gentian. They just roll their eyes and break out the trail mix while he waxes poetic.

But Don's former associates would not believe this scene. In the "man eat man" roofing business in Galveston, Texas, Don supervised guys in toolbelts; flowers were the last thing on his mind.

"I used to walk around and all I saw was roofs; now I walk around looking for flowers," he said. "The people who knew me back in Texas would be shocked. This is the furthest thing from anything I ever thought I'd be doing. It's the rare air, I guess."

A BOI ("born on the island") Galveston native, Don and his wife Cindy began eyeing Colorado in the 1980s, but hurricanes kept yanking people's roofs off and sending him back to the ladder. Finally they discovered Crested Butte in 1987 and lived for their ski vacations: "We'd wait in line for the lift to open in the morning and catch the last chair up at 3:59," he said. "I couldn't have told you the name of a single wildflower."

After both their children graduated and married, the Hempels retired in their early fifties, moved to Crested Butte full time and started hiking and skiing with the Gray Hares, an informal group of just-past-young outdoorspeople. Somewhere up in the rare air, amid the profusion of Crested Butte's wildflowers, Don caught the enthusiasm of Gray Hare flower aficionados Lou Beckman and Angie Kray. He took some courses during Crested Butte's Wildflower Festival, read a few books and hiked with local experts Vinnie Rossignol and Kathy Darrow. Next thing he knew, he had a shelf full of flower books and was spouting Latin names to his amazed friends. He loved how the Latin names often carried coded information about the flowers. The early-season marsh marigold's Latin name, *Psychrophylla leptosepala*, describes it as a cold-loving plant with seven sepals. "It's neat what you can find out just from learning the names," he said.

Soon Don was interrupting conversations, calling his kids and waking up his wife to share enthralling information.

"Honey, listen. This is the neatest thing. There's this legend about monkshood (which I'm sure you know is *Aconitum columbianium* in the Latin). It supposedly came from Aconite, the hill where Hercules fought Cerberus, the three-headed dog. While they were duking it out, Cerberus worked up quite a slobber, and the spittle, which of course was poisonous, sprayed the ground far and wide. Where it landed, monkshood sprouted. That explains why monkshood is so poisonous."

"Fascinating," would come the reply from beneath the pillow beside him. "Tell me more… over breakfast tomorrow morning."

Don found a more appreciative audience when he led tours for the Wildflower Festival. He also found kindred spirits among fellow festival board members and other local wildflower fans by training, vocation or obsession.

Crested Butte earns its official designation as Colorado's wildflower capital with the abundance and variety of flowers that paint its hillsides. Soon Don was fascinated not only by the big, gaudy flowers, but also by the tiny, ground-hugging ones, nicknamed "belly flowers" by their enthusiasts. "When you crawl around looking for itty-bitty things, you find a whole other layer of nature we hardly ever see," he said.

▲ Colorado's state flower, the regal columbine. Photo: Runge

▼ To see and smell: wild roses sweeten the summer air. Photo: Runge

43

Spending hundreds of hours outside, he began to notice nature's amazing adaptations. "Flowers don't just sit there and look beautiful," he said. The black-headed daisy, which pushes through the snow at the first sign of spring, is white on top but black underneath, so it can soak up the warmth of sunlight reflecting off the snow below it.

The aspen sunflower, whose face follows the sun, has developed an ingenious defense against the tetrus flies that lay their eggs in its buds so their maggots can eat its seeds. The sunflower produces a sticky sweet syrup that attracts hordes of ants, deterring the pesky flies from landing. The sky pilot that grows at high altitude, however, needs to attract the flies that are the prime pollinators at its elevation. So it produces an odor stinky to humans but irresistible to flies.

Over the years, Don has also learned a bit about medicinal and edible plants, though other locals specialize in those realms. He knows that glacier lily pods taste like sugar snap peas, sweet cicely like anise, bluebells like raw fish (not so popular, that one) and osha, well, better to think of it as a decongestant than a snack.

Though Don's enthusiasm has hardly rubbed off on his family, he has gathered a following of repeat tour participants. He has identified up to 90 flowers on a single hike, but most enjoys relating the legends, facts and trivia that make the flowers memorable. "Some people come back year after year," he said.

When the snows cover Crested Butte's wild gardens, Don happily trades his hand lens for ski poles, skiing and volunteering at the resort with gusto. But when the sprouts peek through the snow again, he's back at his flower books.

Sometimes Don thinks about his former life with a laugh. "Everything we do here, we didn't do at home. There I'd go down to the beach with a lot of beer and 'veg out.' Here we hike, bike, climb peaks; the mountains are amazing and there's such an active group of people here. It's like living a new life." ✥

▲ A classic wild bouquet in Yankee Boy Basin, starring columbines and bluebells. Photo: Leacock

▶ Sagelands roll toward a distant Gothic Mountain. Photo: Runge

▲▶ The red columbine wears fewer petals but flashier colors than its purple cousin. Photo: Runge

▼▶ Primary colors: Indian paintbrush and lupine in a bed of fresh greens. Photo: Runge

▼▶▶ Monkeyflowers splash yellow on the palette of July. Photo: Runge

▲ Classic Colorado columbine, cozied up with sneezeweed. Photo: Runge

▼ A flower party outside the Finders Keepers cabin. Photo: Runge

▶▶ Lupine, columbine and sunflowers bid farewell to the day on the flanks of Crested Butte Mountain. Photo: Leacock

▲ Sunlight creeps down the Slate River Valley to warm the new day. Photo: Leacock

▶▶ Janae and Ben Pritchett, at home in the wilds.

When you fall in love by alpenglow

Backcountry sweethearts Ben and Janae Pritchett don't
envy their friends' office cubicles.

Ben and Janae Pritchett exchanged their wedding vows (he wearing a tux,
she in a wedding gown and both with bare feet) in a meadow ringed by the Ruby
and Anthracite mountains. How fitting for a romance that took root amid the snow
and wildflowers of Crested Butte's backcountry.

Ben, who leads skiing, biking and climbing trips with Crested Butte
Mountain Guides, and Janae, a teacher and professional athlete, courted not at
movies and concerts, but while huffing up alpine trails on their bikes. They fell in
love not by fancy candlelight but by alpenglow. These days, while most couples hop
on the bus to catch some quick runs at the ski resort, Ben and Janae wake in the
wee hours, strap skins on their skis and climb into the wilds to play on untouched
powder fields.

"Skiing at the resort is about getting more turns, faster, in a safe and predictable environment," Ben said. Backcountry skiing takes time and work, but pays
off with solitude, celebration, surprise and discovery. "It's about quality over quan-
tity; it's more of a journey."

With those descriptions, Ben could easily be comparing the Pritchetts' lives to the lives of their urban friends. The couple is as comfortable in the vast, unpredictable wilderness around Crested Butte as their long-distance buddies are in office cubicles.

"City folks seem largely caught up in routines," Janae said. "Often they don't have time to pursue their true passions. People here in Crested Butte are truly passionate. They make a commitment to do what they love, whether it's art or music or being outdoors."

While urbanites talk about the day's traffic, crime and work hassles, Ben and Janae enthuse about the fox that danced across their ski tracks, the dramatic storm that bequeathed them a double rainbow, the newfound pond that inspired an impromptu swim. "There's a constant sense of adventure in the backcountry," Ben said.

Both Ben and Janae left behind traditional urban childhoods. California girl Janae, a phenomenal athlete and scholar who captained Yale's swim team, came to Crested Butte as an alpine novice, but quickly excelled at every sport she tried. "I wanted to immerse myself in the mountains," she said. "I learned how to ski, how to bike. I can't imagine living here and not wanting to get out and see all these amazing places."

Janae balances outdoor pursuits with teaching math and science at the Crested Butte Community School. In 2005 her middle school students presented her with The Superwoman Award "because she wins every competition there is in Crested Butte." Her recent athletic resumé includes national-level wins in telemarking, snowboarding, mountain biking, triathlons (run/swim/bike combos) and alpine skiing. Even her rivals agree, though, that Janae is powered more by joy than by competitiveness.

As a child, Ben spurned city entertainments in favor of playing outside and "making forts in the compost pile." Drawn to wilder environs, he traded engineering courses at the University of Colorado for nature studies at Western State College. Field work, hiking, skiing and biking acquainted him with the far reaches of the Gunnison Valley, which earned him his jobs with Crested Butte Mountain Guides and the Crested Butte Avalanche Center.

The mountains around Crested Butte are now Ben's office, church and playground. "That's where I go for rejuvenation, spiritual fulfillment and fun," he said.

As a guide, Ben provides a "safety net" for people to venture into the backcountry. "Most of my clients are perfectly capable of picking up a map and figuring

▲ Ascension against the sky. Photo: Ladoulis

it out," he said. "But it feels too foreign to them." People often get fearful when they first lose sight of the car or other signs of civilization, then slowly begin to relax and appreciate the beauty, fragility and power of Crested Butte's wild spaces.

Every outdoor trip, of course, brings its own surprises. "One of the neat things about nature is realizing how small you are and how little control you have," Janae said.

That point struck home while she was conducting research in Yellowstone, walking along and looking down to collect coyote scat, when she suddenly realized she was 50 feet from a grizzly bear "half the size of a Jeep."

"That bear was so beautiful I wanted to watch her. But I was acutely aware that she could kill me in a heartbeat." Janae quietly backed away from the unsuspecting bear, but held on to the memory.

Wildlife studies also led Ben to his most unusual animal encounter. Crawling around in the brush doing bird surveys, he came face to face with a porcupine, just a couple of feet away. He talked soothingly to the spiky beast and reached a peaceful understanding, then suddenly spotted a great horned owl watching him from another nearby bush. "It was wacky. I've spent hundreds of hours walking around the willows, but that is one hour I'll never forget."

Every season holds its own draw for Ben and Janae. Winter is both harder and more rewarding, with is own distinct beauty, silence and solitude: "Snow turns everything into an adventure," Janae said. By contrast, a Crested Butte summer brings moderate temperatures and an "amazingly easy environment," Ben said, but with ready access and more people, "you have to go farther to get that wilderness feel."

After falling in love under the spell of the wild, Ben and Janae intend to live their lives in the same spirit, valuing well-earned discovery over easy routine. They can hardly imagine a better setting for that than Crested Butte, with its vast wild reaches and tiny treasures still left to find.

"That's what I love about this area," Ben said. "There's so much wild space it would take a lifetime to explore it all. It's a great place to encourage discovery."

▲ Scott McDaniel and Carolyn Bird take a beauty break near West Maroon Pass. Photo: Stillo

▼ Two snow-hungry free-heelers head for the shuttle bus early on a powder morning. Photo: Spahn

▲ Near the summit of Crested Butte Mountain, Kasha Rigby and Adam Comey can survey the East River valley toward Gothic. Photo: Stillo

▼ Red Mountain horseback riders Rhonda and David McCay meander through the rich colors and crisp air of autumn. Photo: Stillo

▶▶ Fall scatters a million golden coins along the trail...for those going slow enough to see. Photo: Ladoulis

▲ Life is good. Photo: Spahn

▶▶ Local boys plunge off the Long Lake rope swing during summer's glory days. Photo: Bilow

Growing up outside the box

To my son on his way to the city.

Dear Chris,

I'm trying to get ready. In a few weeks, Michael and I will drop you off at the University of Denver, your new home smack in the middle of the city. Maybe I'll lose my cool then, but right now I'm mostly feeling grateful that I got to be your live-in mom for eighteen years, and that you got to grow up in Crested Butte.

Chris Garren in the city. Hmmm, different. I think of you mostly outside… playing in streambeds, building campfires, celebrating your sixteenth birthday by skiing Mt. Emmons. But I'm sure you will adapt to the city, in part because of what you will take with you from these mountains. You are strong, resourceful, curious and playful. You had all those traits inside you anyway, but being in wild places gave you the chance to know it more deeply.

When we climbed Gothic Mountain just after your seventh birthday, you collapsed in a whiny heap 200 yards below the summit, convinced you couldn't take one more step. Then, somehow, you mustered the energy to trudge to the top, where the whole universe seemingly opened up below in reward. While the grownups lounged and snacked, you scampered around like a happy kid goat. Will a deep part of you remember that in the future when some life circumstance leaves you once again collapsed in a whiny heap? I hope so.

My favorite times with you outside were just hanging out — wading streams, sliding down snowfields, carving sticks, whatever came along. On camping trips, it was fun to watch you go from day one, when you were bored and naked without your Nintendo, to day two, when the natural world teemed with possibilities for play. You learned to use your imagination instead of your remote control.

I also liked the inherent sense of teamwork that came from backpacking. I had the tent stakes and marshmallows; you had the graham crackers and rainfly. Kind of a global metaphor.

Another metaphor: When you were ten, you picked up a big rock to throw, then saw that you had disrupted an entire community of bugs underneath. You gently put the rock back in place. I think your time outside has made you a better neighbor to the beings, big and small, who share your pocket of the planet.

Though mostly I wanted to play, I also had ulterior motives for lugging you outside; it took a little pressure off of me as a parent. You hopefully soaked up things that I didn't know how to teach. I didn't talk so much about spirituality or environmentalism, though they underpinned my life. Maybe being with you in such grand, mystical beauty was my way of letting you forge your own sense of the earth and the divine.

I hope being outside will always remind you that you are part of something larger than the petty tribulations that tend to fill our days inside walls.

Being in wild places with you also let me invest less energy in the authority figure role. In the outdoors, actions reaped their own rewards: if you didn't collect much firewood, you didn't get much fire. I tried not to run around protecting you from possible injury (though I admit I might have prayed a bit), so you climbed and jumped far beyond the limits I would have mistakenly imposed — yet you never even needed stitches. And societal offenses like belching hardly seemed worth a reprimand in the wilds. Was I a slacker-mom outside, or wise beyond my years? Let's call it wisdom. I think the world will give you enough practice following orders. I liked giving you the chance to follow your own instincts, learn your own lessons and test your own limits. Somehow I could give you that gift more easily in Walrod Gulch than in the Cherry Creek Mall.

▲ Four young scholars of rock skipping do lab work out Oh-Be-Joyful.

◀ In the snow days of winter, the simplest mode of transport is the best. Photo: Leacock

Sometimes we felt closest as a family when we were together in the wilds. We slowed down, relaxed and paid attention. I relished the evenings around the fire or in the tent, sharing funny, honest stories and thoughts.

Of course, you changed the way I went into the mountains. As a curious toddler, you reminded me that sometimes it's better to stop trying to get somewhere else and instead just be where you are (even if you haven't actually reached the trailhead yet). Wonder was everywhere to you: yes, wildflowers were pretty, but what about the satisfying splat made by a rock thrown into a fresh cow patty?

You showed me that spontaneity and curiosity were better (though sometimes dirtier) companions than agendas and goals. What an engaging afternoon we had once we ditched our plans to climb a peak in favor of sifting little rodent skeletons out of the dried owl pellets we found near Hasley Pass.

You taught me to disengage my intellect and re-engage my senses. You'd wait patiently while I'd look up some plant name or Michael would photograph some grand vista, then you'd invite us to come splash, smell, dig, throw and climb. Why settle for a theoretical relationship with the earth when we could have a tactile, playful, interactive one?

So off you go now, to learn about rush hour traffic, shopping mall bargains and sports arenas. I hope you will remember deer sightings and coyote howls. And climbing canyon walls and the first time you plunged off the Long Lake rope swing. And being three years old, falling asleep in my lap, warmed by the campfire, the sounds of nature and the quiet voices of people who loved you. Whether you remember or not, those times will always be part of you. Thank goodness.

Love,

Mom

▲ Raven Bryson and her larger-than-average playmates. Photo: Stillo

◀ Mike Martin and his daughter Lucy at play in an ocean of false helibore (a.k.a. skunk cabbage). Photo: Runge

▲ Night music provided by the Poverty Gulch symphony orchestra: stream, frogs and distant coyotes. Photo: Stillo

▼ Riders LuLu Nelson, Jerry and Anna Smith. With so many trails, mountain bikers can choose maximum sweat, wildflowers, vistas or icy stream crossings. Photo: Stillo

▶▶ If you got to be a kid in Crested Butte, you'd celebrate, too. Photo: Ladoulis

▲ Dana Christy and son Tanner doing some outdoor bonding. Photo: Stillo

▲▶ Three Spahn cousins, Jamey, Bailey and Peyton, share the tire swing near Round Mountain's hay fields. Photo: Spahn

▼ At least one July Fourth princess is practicing her parade wave. Photo: Runge

▼▶ Dakota and Montana Wiggins, Dylan Curtiss and Matt Evans ride the wild floaties at the Club at Crested Butte swimming pool. Photo: Ladoulis

▼▶▶ Downhillers and their mountain bikes catch a lift up Crested Butte Mountain. Photo: Ladoulis

▲ The daily alpine light show turns the Slate River to liquid red. Photo: Demerson

▼ Elephant head flowers reward a closer look with their intricate beauties. Photo: Runge

▶▶ A new fawn rests in its grassy cradle. Photo: Runge

▲ Pat Wild riding the rail, Crested Butte style.

Nathan Bilow

Remember to Play

❧

*We know how
to work, but
we specialize
in recess*

▲   Journalist and soccer coach Than Acuff also makes a fetching Miss Mardi Gras. Photo: Ladoulis

▶▶ Kate Seeley and fellow Medieval wenches cavort around the Vinotok harvest bonfire. Photo: Gallaher

Playing dress-up

Delight and fingerpainting don't have to be outgrown here.

I never went to preschool or kindergarten, but I've overcompensated by living in Crested Butte for a quarter century. I don't mean to imply that Crested Butte suffers from immaturity or arrested development; we've just recreated for ourselves some of the joys lost to most American post-kindergarteners.

Say, for example, playing dress-up. As MJ and I browsed through photographs for possible use in this book, we stopped to enjoy a photo series showing wildly costumed characters: hippies, hookers, a giant hot dog....

"Must be Halloween," MJ said.

"Or the Fourth of July... or maybe Vinotok."

"No — look. The mountains in the background are snowy. I'll bet it's Mardi Gras. Or the Red Lady Salvation Ball, or the Golden Marmots."

"Wait... that guy dressed as the Titanic is on telemark skis. It's gotta be the Al Johnson Memorial Uphill-Downhill."

Yes, this town likes to play dress-up. My teenage son's shiny Afro wig shows serious signs of wear, while his handsome sports jacket could well have the price tags still dangling from it. Serious athletes train intently for international-level competitions like the Alley Loop cross-country ski marathon, taking time out only to assemble their clown or nightclub-singer costume ensembles for the big event.

Maybe our urge to don outrageous outfits comes as a balance to eight months of parka wearing. Maybe it's cabin fever, or sensory deprivation here three hours from the nearest mega-mall. Or maybe it just follows from our belief that playfulness doesn't have to be outgrown. Consider the evidence for this belief:

Arts and crafts. Fingerpainting at fifty? No problem. Pat Crow, former arts purveyor at Stepping Stones Children's Center who now directs the Center for the Arts, decided kids shouldn't have all the fun. So she initiated Creativity Salons to bring arts and crafts back into the lives of Crested Butte's grown-ups. Since then, dozens of citizens (many of whom used to consider themselves non artistic) have gathered to paint, make masks, construct collages, draw, fingerpaint and play with clay. "There's no pressure; it's not product oriented," Pat said. "It's about getting your hands dirty and laughing."

Hide and seek. Nobody had to create a venue for this childhood favorite; it's part of life here. Snow hides things; you seek them. Depending on the size of the storm, almost anything left outside can become a playing piece in this game — the snow shovel, trash can, barbecue grill, compact car. True hide-and-seek fanatics can challenge themselves on a higher level through Crested Butte Search and Rescue. As the playing field gets bigger (up to two million acres of wilderness) and the stakes higher (the lost person's survival), the props get cooler: e.g. walkie-talkies, helicopters and search dogs.

Make-believe. An impressive percentage of Crested Butte's residents have donned alter personas via the Mountain Theatre, which lures both professionals and first-timers to the delightful terror of the stage.

Chase. Why do grueling races like the Grand Traverse (hideous all-night backcountry ski trek to Aspen) and the Alley Loop (up to 42 kilometers of Nordic lung torture) draw such avid participants? Maybe it's the childhood thrill of pursuing and being pursued.

Music, movement, games and goofiness. All part of normal adult life in Crested Butte. Bookkeepers and ski instructors take the stage for open-mic night and drumming jam sessions; massage therapists roll up their sleeves for the log-sawing competition. Advancing age is no excuse when it comes to hockey and softball; the average age of the 2005 Gray Hares softball team surpassed the life expectancy in most of the world's countries. And the town has a decidedly different idea of

▲ The Sunshine Girls take a dousing in the "wet zone" of the July Fourth parade. Photo: Ladoulis

▼ Would you hire these guys to lead you into the wilderness? Mountain guides Ian Hatchett and Alan Bernholtz prep — and primp — for the Randonnee Rally. Photo: Ladoulis

decorum. Dignified former mayor and banker Thom Cox will forever be remembered for his ballet in tutu and tights celebrating the opening of the Center for the Arts. Ski executive John Norton once greeted visiting journalists at their conference-opening ceremony wearing only surfer shorts and blazing ski gloves, having set his digits afire to honor the event sponsor, Hotfingers.

Playground time. As befits an adult version of kindergarten, Crested Butte's million-acre-plus play yard has some of the biggest and best playground equipment around… like jungle gyms and slides with 4,000 feet of vertical. Like high-mountain water parks with diving cliffs, rope swings and waterfalls, but no whistle-blowing lifeguards — or other human beings — in sight. Like spectacular hiking and mountain biking trails with more wild mileage than a hundred urban rec-trail systems. Although we didn't invent the bumpersticker that says "He who dies with the most toys wins," we could have; if a car bears a local license plate, it probably also bears a ski, bike or kayak rack.

Now, don't get me wrong. Crested Butte gives its nod to professionalism, high standards, work ethic and responsibility. We attend council meetings, vote, take cookies to school parties and maybe even write inter-office memos like our urban counterparts. We just haven't forgotten the most important lesson of our early schooling: the value of recess.

▲ Betty Bear forgot her Lycra but still leads the pack in the Alley Loop cross-country ski race through town. Photo: Ladoulis

▲ The Butte Box Derby lures speedsters of all persuasions out of the garage onto the streets of Mt. Crested Butte. Photo: Ladoulis

▼ Carousers around the Vinotok bonfire set ablaze the woes of the past to start the year afresh. Photo: Bilow

▶▶ Intent trio Scott Cielinski, Ashton Mabry and Gage Meredith, 30 seconds from launching their competitive biking careers. Photo: Ladoulis

▲ Harvest maiden Gillian Atchley celebrates September's Vinotok Festival. Photo: Gallaher

▲▶ Debonair newspaper editor Edward Stern capitalizes on his uncanny resemblance (at least from the ears up) to television icon Telly Savalas. Photo: Ladoulis

▼ Parade perennial Allen Cox chauffeurs Flauschink royalty Paula Dietrich and Tom Lucci through the paparazzi-lined streets of Crested Butte. Photo: Ladoulis

▼▶ Kansas City Brass musicians turn thin air into big music during their Crested Butte summer sessions. Photo: Gallaher

▼▶▶ Bicyclists tackle the ski slopes during the Wildflower Rush downhill race in Mt. Crested Butte. Photo: Ladoulis

▲   Days like this remind Wendy Fisher why she left the U.S. Ski Team and started skiing for fun again. Photo: Bilow

▶▶   In one week Wendy won the 2005 U.S. Freeskiing Championship and found out she was going to be a mom. Photo: James Lozeau

Back from the dark side

Ski champ Wendy Fisher knows why girls just wanna have fun.

Maybe it was jitters that jiggled Wendy Fisher's innards the morning she launched a 40-foot cliff and powered her way to the 2005 U.S. Freeskiing Championship. Or maybe it was morning sickness.

Wendy and her husband, Woody Lindenmeyr, had no clue she was pregnant until a week after she hoisted the freeskiing trophy. "When I found out, I thought, 'Cool, my kid's already a champion,'" she said.

Few kids will be able to say they co-piloted their mom to a national freeskiing championship in utero. Come to think of it, few kids likely will grow up like Wendy's son or daughter (who is scheduled to make his/her appearance about the same time as this book). I just can't see cliff-jumper Wendy plucking her toddler off the ladder of the playground slide and saying, "Oh, honey, don't try that. You might hurt yourself."

And I'd be sorely disappointed if, some years down the line, Wendy sternly instructed her adolescent, "Just put your nose to the grindstone; you can have fun later."

Wendy is a drop-out from The Grindstone School of Personal Success. Skiing — and life in Crested Butte — have continually shown her that happiness is, indeed, the best medicine — and teacher and motivator and companion.

"Ninety percent of my best competitions, in ski racing and free skiing, were because I was happy," she said. "For me, happiness is a huge part of doing well."

Maybe that's why Wendy's Fish Ski camps for adolescent/teenage girls draw such rave reviews. For much of their time together, Wendy and her campers frolic around Crested Butte Mountain, catching air off little kickers, darting down short-cuts through the trees, and tucking steeps just for the heck of it. They're too busy laughing and whooping to realize they are honing their balance, quickness, skills and confidence with scarcely a hint of the hideous "drill" word.

"It's about opening them up," Wendy said. "They learn to play with obstacles, more speed, different terrain. There's something cool about seeing kids get psyched about skiing."

Not so long ago, Wendy was doing this same thing as a freckle-faced, red-headed sprite chasing her brothers around the slopes of Squaw Valley, California. Skiing, on the mountain or through the racing gates, gave her such joy that she followed her brother to Burke Mountain Academy in Vermont. Though coaches at first doubted the staying power of the tiny dynamo, she scampered her way up the ski ladder: Junior Olympics, Eastern Cup, Nationals, World Cup, U.S. Ski Team. Ranked among the best American skiers in both slalom and giant slalom, she joined the Olympic Ski Team for the '92 Olympics in Albertville, France. A flying crash during training banished her to the medical center, where she watched television coverage of her teammates, highlighted every few minutes by the oft-replayed clip of her dramatic tumble.

The injury gave Wendy time to ponder. Why was she losing her delight on the slopes? "Even as my dreams were coming true, I was getting sadder and more depressed," she said. Eventually, though her coaches thought she would make the next Olympics, she left the team. A ski scholarship brought her to Sierra Nevada College, where she racked up racing victories but felt "burnt to a crisp." Skiing was no longer about goofing off, hanging out with friends, flying freely down the slopes; it was about pressure, training, race times. "I was lost. Skiing was all I knew, but I wasn't having a good time," she said. "I crumbled."

Luckily, extreme skiing pioneer Kim Reichhelm recognized Wendy's all-too-familiar symptoms when they met at a celebrity ski event. A fellow refugee from the rigid pressure of the U.S. Ski Team, Kim invited Wendy to visit her in Crested

▲ Joy in motion: Pat Wild on a powder day. Photo: Bilow

Butte, with its gnarly ski mountain and healthy culture of play. Wendy dropped by…
and stayed. In Crested Butte, skiing once again meant bashing around trees, steeps,
chutes and cliffs with the local rowdies (one of whom would become her husband).
Her childhood *joie de skiing* bounced back with vigor.

Three weeks later, friends talked Wendy into entering the U.S. Freeskiing
Championships, where she danced her way to third place and into a career she'd
never imagined. The next few years brought a succession of national and interna-
tional freeskiing titles, film contracts with Matchstick Productions and Warren
Miller, sponsorships, her own ski clinics and, most importantly, big fun on Crested
Butte's slopes.

"It blew me away how cool the freeskiing extremes were. And nerve wrack-
ing," she said. "In ski racing, they tell you where to go; you just have to be quick. In
freeskiing, you have to figure out your lines, all the nooks and crannies. There's a
kind of showmanship aspect to the race. You can hear people roaring when they're
psyched about your run."

True to her resolve to "keep it fun," Wendy stopped competing in the U.S.
Freeskiing Championships when she found herself feeling pressured and fretful.
"Success isn't worth being miserable," she said. But in 2005, after a four-year break,
she again entered and won. "I just felt good," she said. "This mountain makes you a
great skier. I still find myself improving, getting quicker, agile, fluid and smooth."

Wendy hopes to ski professionally for a few years after her child is born, then
ease her career and life in new directions. Skiing will take on yet another role in her
life with a new little companion to chase her around the mountain. Life lessons, a
child and Crested Butte's culture will hopefully remind her to keep the fun quo-
tient high.

"A lot of people here in Crested Butte work to play. There's nothing wrong
with that. It's better than working so hard that there's no way to enjoy the rewards
except by buying things. People get too scared to get out of their miserable routines, until it starts being part of their life to not have fun. Skiing wouldn't let me
do that; if I wasn't happy, I didn't perform. It was a good thing to learn."

▲ Elk Avenue turns into a wild big-air ski jump during the annual Winter Carnival. Photo: J.C. Leacock

▼ Young tubing hill fans Selina and Marlida Mear fly their way down the slopes. Photo: Stillo

▲ Jason Pogoloff grabs a front side indy on Crested Butte's halfpipe. Photo: Bilow

▲ Three generations on skis: Sarah McAllister celebrates a family ski day with her daughter Ellie and dad Jack. Photo: Stillo

▲ Sometimes reaching the goal is worth breaking a new trail. Photo: Leacock

▲▶ Daylight fades like cosmic theater lights dimming in deference to the moon's grand entrance. Photo: Demerson

▼ More Nordic trails than paved roads? Skiers can skim more than 50 kilometers of groomed trails lacing Crested Butte's backyard. Photo: Stillo

▼▶ Beauty notwithstanding, Rod Cesario must be one dedicated fisherman. Photo: Stillo

▼▶▶ Light-footed Michelle Russell. Photo: Stillo

▲ Abby Leinsdorf has performed as far away as Italy but still likes the Center for the Arts, with her friends in the audience. Photo: Stillo

▶▶ Keepers of culture: Center for the Arts director Pat Crow (left) and former director Patricia Dawson. Photo: Bilow

Spanky as arts mentor

Remembering the pure delight of putting on a show.

Pat Crow's career path may have been set the day her childhood neighbors built a stage in their playroom. There she spent long, happy hours bossing around her brothers and friends to enact their latest drama. She understood the thrill of the television rascals on "Spanky and Our Gang" when they clapped their hands together and exclaimed, "Oh! Let's put on a show!" At that moment, the excitement wasn't about the audience, the income or the reviews, but purely about the joy of creating the show.

Today, as the director of Crested Butte's Center for the Arts, Pat's life work revolves around a bigger stage, with a $350,000 budget and performers as famous as Taj Mahal. But her mentor hasn't changed; in the midst of fundraising campaigns, committee vision statements and performer fee negotiations, she tries to hear Spanky's delighted voice: "Oh! Let's put on a show!"

Growing up in the rural outskirts of Philadelphia, Pat and her buddies plumbed television for plots to re-enact. "I remember one story involved a scorpion sting that resulted in a painful death," she said. "We did that one over and over. Yes, there was a lot of drama in my early life. I was very shy, but I liked to boss people around, so directing was a natural progression."

The propensity later crept into Pat's life as a high school social studies teacher in Tennessee, where she taught partly through role-playing and directed the school's 1976 bi-centennial gala. With that finale, she packed up her car and headed west toward Montana, but kept hearing about some lively little community called Crested Butte. So she stopped by, a detour that has so far lasted three decades.

"My car broke down and Myles Arber offered me a job working the business beat for the *Crested Butte Chronicle*," she said. As she did stints at the newspaper, Crested Butte Printing, her own ad agency and Stepping Stones Children's Center, the stage worked its way back into Pat's life.

"I got to know Eric Ross (former Crested Butte Mountain Theatre director) when he'd come into the print shop, pull these ratty bits of scribbled-on paper out of his pockets, and say, 'Can you make a poster out of this?' One day I was walking by the theater and Eric grabbed me. 'We've having auditions; come upstairs right now.' I got a part in 'The Good Doctor' — as did every person who auditioned."

Soon Pat was reliving her childhood glory days, helping create dramas and comedies on the Mountain Theatre stage, though seldom in the spotlight herself.

"Back then we weren't jocks; that was before mountain biking," she said. "Music and theater were the way we all came together. We were dance-in-the-woods flower children, not X Gamers."

Friends recruited Pat to the Mountain Theatre board, then to the job of director during a pivotal transition. True to the "Spanky and Our Gang" philosophy, the theater had focused on productions primarily to challenge and engage the cast, crew and community. From tents in the park to the Old Town Hall with its splintery wooden bleachers and no backstage plumbing, Mountain Theatre plays drew a large percentage of Crested Butte's tiny population to participate or spectate. "We put on shows for ourselves," Pat said. "They were for people here to watch, be in and direct."

Then theater mainstays began envisioning bigger possibilities. "We started thinking, 'Imagine what we could do if we had a real stage and lights and didn't have to pee in a can.' That creates a situation where money becomes important, so you begin to produce things partly for the income. It makes your choices different," Pat said.

That ambitious wave swept through the whole cultural scene in Crested Butte. In 1986-87, residents, foundations, local businesses and second homeowners rallied behind a campaign to remodel the old county shop building into a performing arts center. The new Center for the Arts went far beyond the much-coveted

▲ Next time theater veteran Eric Ross should help duet partner Sean Riley with his makeup. If you call 911 and Sean shows up, don't worry; he makes a better EMT than drag queen. Photo: Ladoulis

▼ Bruce Hayes, Crested Butte's own music man. Photo: Gallaher

lights and bathrooms (though for a couple of years until the plumbing was refined, signs asked audiences to refrain from flushing during performances). With its relatively sophisticated sound and lighting, plush seating, lobby and visual arts gallery, the facility grew into a true arts center.

After Pat Crow took over from Center director Patricia Dawson in 1992, she helped shape the cultural life of Crested Butte. With so many new possibilities, she found herself balancing various community ambitions with the Spanky School of Joyful Performing. The Center stage was soon shared by renowned professional dancers and charming, fumble-footed preschoolers beaming in their new tutus. Commanding divas from the Metropolitan Opera have performed one week, followed the next by ski instructors and restaurateurs trembling through their first-ever speaking roles.

The Center presents a variety of shows, as well as providing the venue for user groups such as Dansummer, the Crested Butte Music Festival, Mountain Theatre, Reel Fest, Creative Arts Institute and other presenters. Pat has brought in performances as diverse as the Fred Garbo Inflatable Theater, Aspen-Santa Fe Ballet, Glenn Miller Orchestra and Los Lobos. She instigated free outdoor Alpenglow concerts, with toddlers frolicking among picnickers' blankets in the park. The Center also hosts art exhibits and free-form Creativity Salons, inviting non-artists to play with paint, scissors and other media. Pat loves those salons: "I'd burn out if I couldn't play," she said.

These days Crested Butte wavers on the cusp of change, Pat senses. She hopes the town might some day rank among the top 100 art towns in the country, with a thriving community of visual and performing artists. A Crested Butte Arts and Recreation group recently presented proposals to build a new performance facility and revamp the existing building. Organizations like the Crested Butte Music Festival envision local music and dance schools, international reputations and expanded arts tourism.

Easy as it is to get swept up, Pat anchors the new visions with Crested Butte's cultural roots. "I hope we always remember this is for the community," she said. Even as she values the diverse and renowned performers who bring their gifts to Crested Butte, she remembers the power of art on the community level: bringing people together across socioeconomic lines to challenge themselves and share the pure delight of putting on a show.

▲ The Center's Alpenglow concerts in the park have spurred a new level of picnicking sophistication. Photo: Demerson

◀ Nobody's gonna mess with Tuck, in western tough-guy regalia for Sean Guerrero's newest movie venture. Photo: Gallaher

◀◀ Allegra "Pi" Duval has dancing in her blood. Photo: Bilow

▲ Shaun Horne takes plein-air painting to an extreme. Photo: Gallaher

▲▶ Mary Tuck, actress, director, artist and hostess of ladies' "wig nights." Photo: Ladoulis

▼ Performers Paul Gallaher and Bill Dowell, pillars of Crested Butte's thriving musical subculture. Photo: Stillo

▼▶ Elk Avenue turns into a giant open-air gallery for the Festival of the Arts, generally held the first weekend in August. Photo: Stillo

▼▶▶ The Crested Butte School of Dance has inspired two decades worth of dancers. Photo: Bilow

▲ Snow date: Darlene and Tim Egelhoff, Skye and Heidi head to the slopes while the snowflakes continue to fall. Photo: Stillo

▶▶ Annie and Bill Coburn, collectors of gear, adventures and kids. Photo: Ladoulis

The family that plays together

The Coburns: Happiness is four kids and a garage full of toys.

"We don't stop playing because we grow old; we grow old because we stop playing." If Oliver Wendell Holmes' quote is true, Bill and Annie Coburn might stay young for a very long time.

Even with four kids and a thriving business, the Coburns play as devotedly as ski bums half their age. Santa always knows what to deliver to the Coburn household: more toys. A barn down valley shelters their duckies (inflatable kayaks), raft and snowmobiles, and their garage holds backpacks, skis (cross-country, alpine and skate), mountain bikes, tents, snowshoes, shotguns and rifles, ice skates and hockey gear, fishing rods (Bill won't admit how many), sleds, golf clubs and snowboards.

"Everything fits but the cars," Annie said.

One year Santa brought paintball guns, gear and armor for Bill, Annie and their three teens (their youngest child was still a toddler). Trips to the family cabin in Tincup, a semi-ghost town near Crested Butte, turned into paintball extravaganzas. "The kids love to shoot me," Annie said.

Bill and Annie fell in love as fun-spirited classmates during their University of Colorado days. In 1985, after many hiking, camping and ski outings from their Boulder home, they took on bigger adventures, setting out to climb all 54 of Colorado's fourteeners (peaks over 14,000 feet in elevation). Bill finished in 1988;

Annie has only four more to go. "She was pregnant so much that I got way ahead," Bill said.

As the Coburn kids grew, the family spent several weeks each summer at their Tincup cabin, which has been in Bill's family for four generations. The summer vacation almost always included a week in Crested Butte. "We wanted to instill western values in the kids," Bill said. They taught Willy, Gracie and Emma how to build a fire, start a snowmobile, tie a fly and clean a gun. "We did it for them, and for us... hoping they wouldn't grow up and relocate to some place like Florida," Bill said.

In 1998, the Coburns decided to spend a year in Crested Butte, savoring all the activities they'd had to cram into their annual vacations.

"It was our year to go for it," Annie said. "Then, after that winter, we said, 'Gosh, we can't not do that again.' The Crested Butte school was awesome, the kids made great friends and we had so much fun. So our one-year sabbatical turned into forever."

During their "go for it" year, the Coburns reaffirmed the value of playing outdoors, especially in Crested Butte, with endless trails, streams, a ski resort and five mountain wilderness areas within a few minutes of their home. "Crested Butte is the most perfect spot in Colorado as far as proximity to the things we like to do," Annie said.

She generally finds "a fun little adventure" every day: mountain biking, hiking, golfing, snowshoeing or skiing on Nordic or alpine skis. "Instead of being stuck going to a health club, I go right out the door, where it's so beautiful," she said. "I think having so much fun makes you happier, more relaxed, attuned and alert. You keep things in perspective."

In between presiding over Coburn Development and serving as a Crested Butte Town Council member, Bill heads outside as often as possible. He celebrated Fathers Day 2005 by kayaking with his daughters and then playing golf with his older son. He and Annie often end their active summer days in the dugout of Pitsker Field as valued players on the Mamas and Papas softball team. Bill logs about forty ski days most winters, to Annie's seventy. But his passion, indisputably, is fly fishing.

"I can stand in water all day and not catch anything and be perfectly happy. It's whatever the stream yields. It's very dynamic, never the same. There's always some little adventure, and of course you're always in a beautiful place." He added, "I've fished in South America, Russia, Alaska, Montana, Idaho and all around Colorado, and I'd still put Gunnison County up against the best of them. You've got

▲ Imagine: No remote control in sight, and nobody's even missing it. Photo: Stillo

◄ Boredom's not an option on a whitewater ride down the upper Taylor. Photo: Stillo

these big rivers that you can follow up to the most obscure little creeks, where there's not a sign of another human."

"Not like a lake with a can of worms and a bunch of people in lawn chairs," Annie added.

Bill and Annie trek into the mountains for longer backpacking trips several times each summer, often climbing a fourteener. They've survived some adventures along the way, like following mountain goats up a treacherous, unmarked route on South Maroon peak. Their occasional scares have come mainly from lightning in high, exposed places.

"One time we were running down this mountain; lightning was hitting below us, above us, everywhere," Bill recalled. "We kissed each other and split up to go in different directions, so the kids would only lose one parent if the lightning hit too close."

After moving to Crested Butte, the Coburns practiced kayaking and rafting, learned to skate ski, began hunting and then shooting chukar and pheasant. How many women get shotguns for their 40th birthdays?

Crested Butte also inspired the birth of little Joe, ten years younger than his nearest sibling. Without the time-consuming driving and hassles of the city, "We had so much more capacity in our lives here," Bill said. "I started hinting about another baby, and Joe was conceived on a fishing/backpacking trip to the Raggeds."

Though Annie favors skiing and Bill loves fishing, neither claims a favorite Crested Butte season.

"Winter has this coziness," Annie said. "There's nothing like skiing under that bold blue sky. It's so bracing. Then after you ski or whatever, you come back to your warm, cozy house. Summer's almost the opposite; the weather is so gentle and the days are so long, you just go and go until you drop."

"Maybe fall is the best," Bill added. "There's hunting and great fishing, the days are crisp and beautiful, and the weather is predictable. And there aren't as many people around. Or maybe the best thing is just that we have these distinct seasons."

Bill and Annie keep an ongoing list of peaks they have yet to climb, trails to ride, loops to hike, streams to raft, slopes to ski and fishing spots to find. "There are almost endless possibilities here," Bill said. "I'm never leaving. It's perfect."

▲ Bonding experience: Three-legged races down Elk Avenue during the Winter Carnival. Photo: Bilow

▼ The challenging holes at the Club at Crested Butte keep golf pro John Kuzina on his game. Photo: Stillo

▲ Hundreds of bikers set up temporary housekeeping on the school soccer field during the Bike Tour of Colorado. Photo: Bilow

▼ Chris Hanna, ex football guy turned deft fly fisherman. Photo: Ladoulis

▶▶ Dynamic skier Jay Prentiss dances with snow. Photo: Bilow

▲ Mike Martin outpaces an afternoon shower on the Snodgrass trail. Photo: Runge

▲▶ Referee Justin encourages budding ice fanatics Sam and Morgan. Photo: Stillo

▼▶ Backcountry paragliding: climb up, float down. Photo: Gallaher

▼▶▶ Bradley Richmond rodeos her kayak down the Taylor River. Photo: Stillo

▼▶▶▶ Who really smiles while they're running? Maybe Susan Bardeen on a sparkling autumn day. Photo: Stillo

▲ Early morning with the world at your feet: Time to think great thoughts… or get your ears scratched.

The Ways We Live

Roots, quirks and gifts along the road less traveled

JC Leacock

▲ To Brad Morton digging out is hard work; to Angel it's a cool new doggie game. Photo: Stillo

▶▶ Graham Ullrich gives his aging buddy Toby a last joy ride in the Bridges of the Butte 24-Hour Townie Tour. Photo: Ladoulis

The gift of doggie obituaries

Sure, Crested Butte citizens live by the book — after they edit it a little.

Not one of my college journalism courses covered canine obituaries. But that's okay. Most of Crested Butte's doggie obits are written not by pros but by the dogs' masters — poignant little tributes, often written as letters to the dear departed (maybe dogs can read in the afterlife) and accompanied by favorite family snapshots.

These doggie obits used to drive me crazy. When I arrived here in 1981, my main arrogance was an honors degree from a top journalism school, the University of Texas. When I first saw the two (yes, two) Crested Butte newspapers, the *Chronicle* and the *Pilot*, I groaned. The articles resembled nothing in my journalism texts; it was Mr. Cox in this paragraph, Tom or Thom in the next and "the illustrious mustachioed mayor" in the middle of the story, where the news lead might finally make its relaxed appearance. Rambling chronological news accounts would have followed naturally from the entrée "Dear Diary...".

Still, for all my journalistic disdain, it took me three weeks to work up the courage to enter the tiny, leaning Pilot building (then on Elk Avenue beside the post office, moved in the mid 1980s to the alley behind the P.O.). When I walked in, editor Lee Ervin didn't bother to remove his feet from the well-littered desktop, moving only to flick his roll-your-own cigarette ash in the general direction of a half-empty longneck.

"Hi, I'm Sandy Fails, I have a journalism degree and several years experience..." I began.

"What are you doing tonight?" Lee's sandpapered voice sounded rougher than he looked, which is saying a lot.

"I beg your pardon?"

"Want to cover the Mt. Crested Butte Town Council meeting?"

Aha. I'd already bowled him over with my credentials, to be entrusted so quickly with such a critical assignment. (Thankfully, I didn't yet know that Lee and everyone else on the loosely called "staff" in those days hated the Mt. Crested Butte Town Council meetings, or that Lee would send just about any gullible, English-speaking newcomer to cover them.)

I eagerly studied the beer-stained agenda Lee excavated from a random pile on his desk, changed into my best jeans, took copious notes at the meeting, and early the next day turned in to Lee a neatly typed, textbook-flawless, pyramid-style news story. He glanced over it, tossed it into the typesetting pile, and said, "Uh, well, maybe we'll try you on features."

Insulted though I was at the time, I have to say thanks to Lee in retrospect. Feature writing was my first real ticket into the rich and quirky mix of Crested Butte. For the next few years I interviewed and wrote features on anyone who captured my fancy: oldtimers Teeny Tezak and Grace Arnott, pianist/mountaineer Steve Monfredo, preschooler Molly Gifford, recently deposed mayor turned state politician W Mitchell, lively octagenarian biologist Harriet Barclay and dozens of other fascinating individuals.

Feature writing bought me admission to a new experience every week: the backstage mischief during a Mountain Theatre production in the Old Town Hall, a snowmobile excursion with John Biro and his fellow Irwin ruffians, a day banding birds at the Rocky Mountain Biological Lab, a life-threatening raft trip, a seat with the snowcat drivers on their midnight slope-grooming rounds, an invitation to the oldtimers' annual pig roast, even a session at Mary Volk's house with Theo, the "community of spirits" that spoke through a visiting medium.

Through feature writing I grew to love Crested Butte, with all its textures, personalities and feistiness. I also (gradually) learned to lighten up. I broke the rules of *The New York Times Style Book*, using the most comfortable rather than most prop-

▲ Well, the sign doesn't say anything about cows. Photo: Demerson

■ When eight feet of snow falls in one storm, you have to get creative about where to put it all. Photo: Gallaher

▼ Elk Avenue after the fall... of snow. Photo: Leacock

115

er names for my subjects (Botsie just didn't work as "Rudolph Spritzer"; Tuck could only be called "Tuck"). I discovered that Crested Butte was sometimes best captured with irreverent humor or unabashed sentimentality rather than professional objectivity. I learned to have fun with my writing.

Meanwhile, the two newspapers (eventually combined into one) scripted their own small-scale journalistic soap opera, with a parade of mergers, mutinies, cooperatives and characters. My favorite times were those when the paper was sharp and attentive but with a quirky edge, when people eagerly grabbed the new issue each week to be entertained as well as informed. Of course the escapades occasionally offended those who were, like me, fresh from the city, like the one person who was outraged when the modesty tape slipped askew on the two-decades-old "Guess Who" photo of a svelte — and topless — Adele Bachman.

I watched with alternating pride and bemusement as the newspaper rollercoastered through its permutations. I like to think I contributed over the years with my deepening affection for the town and delight in writing about it. These days (having jumped ship to the *Crested Butte Magazine*), I write only occasionally for the *Crested Butte News*, the current incarnation of the town newspaper. The young, spirited *News* staffers take the Mt. Crested Butte Town Council meetings a lot more seriously than did Lee a couple of decades ago; in 2005, the paper won 11 Colorado Press Association awards, more than any other newspaper in its size category. But the staff still has fun, and you can still open those pages and see comic photos, birthday listings and, yes, canine memorials.

Recently I realized (once again) how much Crested Butte has changed me when I stumbled across a particularly charming photo of my golden retriever Luke and found myself thinking, "Oh, that would make such a cute photo for the paper when he dies." Yes, I was pondering the missive that must surely be written for such a beloved character in the lives of my family and friends. A doggie obituary. What does it mean?

I think it means that Crested Butte has taught me to forsake certain societal (and even journalistic) rules in favor of what I really care about. A proper education corrupted... another Crested Butte success story.

▲ The running of the ducks. The Rotary Club's 2005 Rubber Ducky Race sent 4,000 ducks down Coal Creek to the enthusiastically staffed finish line at Totem Pole Park. Photo: Ladoulis

◄ Smokey Moore, at ease during the Mountain Man Rendezvous. Photo: Bilow

◄◄ Hipster realtor Jim Barefield gets down with some hula action. Photo: Ladoulis

▲ Early risers on a powder morning: skiers, snowboarders and shovelers. Photo: Ladoulis

▲ Elk Avenue commuter Sami Corn shows common symptoms of post-storm euphoria. Photo: Ladoulis

◄ Michael Helland and Margot Levy, at the tail end of the July Fourth parade, prove that town council members do indeed have to deal with a certain amount of crap. Photo: Ladoulis

▲ As one Alpenglow concert fan said, "It's like a town party every Monday." Photo: Ladoulis

▲ Buck takes Ella Fahrlander for a meadowlands jaunt. Photo: Runge

▲ Sandy Leinsdorf, as a child on the Allen ranch (right) and as president of the Crested Butte Land Trust. Current photo: Demerson

Rooted in the land

Sandy Leinsdorf traded chicken feed for land conservation.

Sandy Allen Leinsdorf hasn't fed a chicken in three decades. She's found a tidier way to work on behalf of the valley's furred and feathered residents.

Sandy grew up, a shy little girl, on the Allen ranch near Jack's Cabin south of Crested Butte. Today, Sandy lives in town and her shyness has gone the way of her pigtails. While her cousin's family runs the ranch, she serves as the gracious and articulate president of the Crested Butte Land Trust, one of the most effective land preservation bodies in the state.

Sandy labors hard for the Land Trust, not only because growing up on a ranch taught her to labor hard, but also because she cares so deeply. While her fellow board members also respect the open spaces they strive to protect, Sandy knows first hand the value of the land and the heritage it represents.

"I still feel very connected to the land," she said. "When you're raised on a ranch, you don't really lose that."

Throughout Sandy's childhood, the land was her family's home, livelihood, playground and legacy. Grandparents, aunts, uncles and cousins pitched in together on the various Allen homesteads in the valley.

"We never took a vacation; ranchers work every day," she said. "I think we took a vacation drive through Colorado once."

Their tasks shifted with the seasons of ranching: calving, haying, etc.

"We always had chores: feeding the chickens, bringing in the cows, cooking for the haying crews. The women worked hard on the ranch as well as the men," Sandy said. "But it was a happy childhood. Working as children has its rewards later, in work ethic and the ability to be responsible and self-reliant."

When she grew up, Sandy left her small, safe circle of family, following friends first to Boston, then to Oregon. The city was both fascinating and shocking after life on the ranch. "Our apartment superintendent got furious because we didn't lock our doors," she recalled. "We were really naïve."

After three years, Sandy headed home to the mountains and worked for the Verzuh Agency in Gunnison, where she met client and beau-to-be David Leinsdorf. Their backgrounds were a study in contrast; David, an attorney and pilot, graduated from Columbia Law School and worked for Ralph Nader at a burn-out pace before seeking respite in the mountains.

"I thought it was great that he wasn't a local homespun guy," Sandy said. "He was interesting to me partly because we were so different."

After Sandy and David married and had children, Sandy quit work and got involved with community causes like the school. When Crested Butte Land Trust officials asked her to join their board of directors, "it seemed like a natural fit," she said. Some of the primary landowners in the valley were the ranchers that Sandy had known all her life, and she understood their struggles to maintain their lands and lifestyle.

"Ranchers don't label themselves as environmentalists, but they protect the environment in ways that others cannot," she said.

Local ranches are threatened by rising real estate prices and property taxes, hassles from increased population and development around them, and high costs of fuel and equipment, Sandy said. "It's very tough for these ranchers; they often have to sell some of their land to pay for improvements to their operations."

Organizations like the Crested Butte Land Trust and the Gunnison Ranchland Conservation Legacy can help ranchers by buying the development rights to some or all of their land, giving them much-needed cash and significant tax benefits while preserving the open land in perpetuity. Having ranchers involved in the organizations strengthens the landowners' trust, Sandy said.

Unlike many of her Land Trust associates, Sandy's history in the valley dates back before tourism was its sustaining economy. Her family lived here when Crested Butte was primarily a mining town, and they witnessed the tough times when the

▲ A bovine version of a hard day at the office. Photo: Spahn

mines closed, the schools shut down and the economy virtually collapsed. Sandy remembers the hard transition when long-haired, city-reared young people moved in and raised the hackles of the oldtimers, then the slow shift to a tourism economy with rising costs of living and real estate. Today, while Crested Butte attracts its annual influx of energetic young people, it is anchored by a strong community of long-time residents, families and second homeowners.

In many ways, Sandy's life reflects the evolution of the valley. She and David live in a comfortably affluent neighborhood just uphill from downtown Crested Butte, where their two children, Abby and Joe, enjoyed a childhood very different from Sandy's. "One of the biggest limitations of growing up on the ranch, 16 miles from anywhere, was the lack of social exposure. If you're introverted anyway, you get really introverted out there," she said. "Growing up in town, our kids are so relaxed and comfortable in people situations. They've had the opportunity to explore their interests — sports, recreation, dance. Their childhoods have had their own healthiness."

Similarly, Sandy feels the immense change in the valley during her lifetime "is not all for the worse; much of it is for the better. We will continue to change; I hope we do it wisely."

Sandy stays connected to the family ranch via her cousin, Curtis Allen, who grew up on the original Allen homestead out Ohio Creek. Curtis and his wife Helen both earned degrees in agriculture before taking on the Allen family ranches. From May through October, Helen runs their cattle on federal grazing leases and private property out Washington Gulch and Oh-Be-Joyful. While she spends the summer living in a small trailer in the wilds and moving the cattle around to avoid overgrazing their summer pastures, the rest of the family focuses on getting in the hay crop back at home.

Sandy often rides with Helen to move the cattle from the ranch to the summer grazing leases and back again.

"Helen is a full-on rancher," Sandy said. "She's strong and hearty and very capable."

Sitting astride a horse, herding the cows through spectacular alpine landscapes, gives more meaning to the work Sandy does inside office walls, forging the logistical and strategic groundwork for land conservation.

"I don't miss living on the ranch, or doing the chores," she said. "But being out there makes me glad I can do something to protect the land and my family's heritage."

▲   Rush hour, cowboy style, out Brush Creek Road. Photo: Bilow

◀   Good water, weather and soil grow some of the best hay in the West. Photo: Stillo

◀◀   Home-grown ranch hand Cody Ray. Photo: Spahn

▲ Barns like this one near Jack's Cabin remind passersby that ranchers still graze cattle, grow hay and preserve the wide-open valley floor. Photo: Bilow

▼ A good day to be a cow. Photo: Stillo

▶▶ Beyond romantic images, ranching generally means hard work for little money; the payoff comes partly in a rich connection to the land. Photo: Spahn

▲ Lake Irwin west of Crested Butte: tourist playground by summer and roadless retreat by winter. Photo: Gallaher

▶▶ John Biro in front of his solar-powered log home at the Irwin townsite. Photo: Gallaher

Life on the road less plowed

John Biro, Irwin's unofficial sheriff, mayor and social director.

John Biro handed the movie box to Bonnie Chlipala at the counter of the Flying Petito Sisters Video Store. She turned to get the video off the shelf, then looked back over her shoulder at Biro, the most famed of the Irwin ruffians.

"You know this has subtitles…"

"Yeah, we like to watch a good foreign film before we rape and pillage," Biro replied.

John Biro is unofficially regarded as the mayor, sheriff and census-taker of Irwin, a tiny, snowbound, off-the-grid community near Lake Irwin, ten miles west of Crested Butte. Summer brings a passel of neighbors, but only a few stay after winter's first snowfalls shut down the road. During some years, Biro, in his self-built, solar-powered log house, has been the only winter resident.

"I came here to camp when I was 25," said Biro. "I'm still here and I'm still camping."

While Crested Butte has been gentrified, Irwin holds to its rowdy reputation, as Biro recently discussed.

"People in town have this fantasy of living up here," he said. "There's this myth that we're up here partying all night, having orgies and drinking a lot."

"Is it true?"

"What day?"

Biro generously offered overnight accommodations for any young female journalist who might want to investigate. "I'm between wives," he explained, having bid adieu to spouse number four ten years ago. "I used to get married a lot. I'm trying to quit. Cigarette smoking is next."

The Irwin culture has mellowed, he admitted, since the days when the Irwin Lodge bar was the center of a rough and ready social scene. (The lodge closed in 2003 for massive remodeling.) But Irwin community ties remain strong, especially in the winter with huge snowfalls and no plowed roads, phones or "imported utilities."

"There's a strong sense of community because it can be life or death up here," he said. "You can knock on any door, day or night, and if you need help, you'll get it. We might not all see eye to eye, but when we all got snowed in in January two years in a row, we raided each other's movies and libraries and mooched each other's groceries."

The snowmobile commute between Irwin and Crested Butte runs a "gauntlet of avalanches" during storm cycles, he said. He once took twelve hours to make the eight-mile trip home during a blizzard, an epic that involved taking apart his snowmobile carburetor, boot packing the trail a few dozen yards at a time as snow fell like down from a million busted pillows, and getting temporarily lost in armpit-deep powder after he finally abandoned his snowmobile in favor of walking.

Then there was the 1996 "inadvertent air" Biro caught, snowmobiling off a cliff on Red Lady. "I shoved my femur through my ass. That hurt."

Avalanches have "pushed me around and knocked the shit out of me," he added. "One time Jeff Brekke, Doug Buzzel, Jeff Halford, Jan Runge and I all got a ride skiing; we had nightmares for a year. The thought of getting buried alive has an edge to it."

Life at Irwin in general has an edge to it. "It gets kind of weird," Biro said. "From my deck I can look in three different directions and see where friends were killed."

Several more people might have died without Biro's famous rescues. His strangest act of heroism came in late February 1993, when he joined eight friends gathered at Mark Hochradle's house to play games. One woman went to sleep early, complaining of a migraine; another acted inordinately drunk; finally they all started "getting loopy" and passing out. Unknown to them, the 400 inches of snow at Irwin had blocked the ventilation to a generator under the deck, and undetected carbon

▲ Kochevars Saloon: Hosting oldtimers, polka bands and bridge club ladies for as long as anyone can remember. Photo: Bilow

monoxide fumes were poisoning them.

At about 2 a.m. Biro regained consciousness after an "other-worldly experience with the Grim Reaper" and realized they were dying. "When I sat up, I was a carbon monoxide expert," he said. Sick and intoxicated by the fumes, he crawled around, opened windows, yelled his companions awake and did rescue breathing when various people stopped breathing on their own. Finally Biro and Hochradle managed to radio the Irwin Lodge at 4 a.m., catching night owl Jade Hyslop, who alerted three EMTs staying at the lodge. When they labored their way through the snow to the house, they found "a pile of bodies and people crawling to each other checking for vital signs and doing rescue breathing," Biro said. Two of the victims couldn't breathe on their own for several hours. Miraculously, all survived.

Biro's heroics made him the topic of an April Fools story in the *Chronicle & Pilot* newspaper, wherein he saves the lives of 40 skiers, a busload of orphans and nuns, and his dog Spot in the course of an ordinary day. These days, Biro laughs at being elevated to icon status, which has been reinforced by the "odd synchronicity" of stumbling so often on desperate people in need of a lift or a spark plug.

"Here's how easy this hero business is," he said. "Me and another guy were coming back toward Irwin on our snowmobiles and saw tracks going into the pond. We looked down where the ice had broken through, and I said, 'Does that look like Kirk the Jerk's snowmobile?' Sure enough, we look up and there is Kirk buck naked on my deck, waving my fifth of Southern Comfort and yelling, 'You saved my life.'"

In contrast to Biro's crusty persona, neighbor Ashleigh Garmon describes him also as the mother hen of Irwin. Biro likes to take care of people, gossip, socialize and attend cultural events more avidly than your typical mountain man, said Ashley, who works at the Center for the Arts.

Biro's compact log home, a.k.a. "Hotel Slednecks," also bucks expectations of a mountain man bachelor pad, with its pampered houseplants, resident cat and immaculate condition. The house looks over its valley like a treehouse, above a snowmobile fix-it shop that is equally immaculate beneath the gaze of its girly posters. In his wild environs, Biro has carved out comforts like a tiny but flawless patch of lawn, goldfish pond and wood-fired hot tub.

Though he used to tell his snowmobile guiding clients that he was born on an Indian reservation, Biro actually grew up in the suburbs of Ohio. He ran away from home at 19. Biro hit Paonia after departing the second Rainbow Festival and

Snow, woodpile, more snow: the timeless refrain of a Crested Butte winter. Top and bottom photos: Leacock. Middle photo: Demerson

"did the Mr. Natural thing" there for a while, then headed to Crested Butte to work for Amax in 1979. At Irwin, he met Forest Queen miner (and "saint") John Hahn, who offered him cheap housing. In the decades since, Biro has "done whatever it takes to survive": e.g. construction, welding, firewood gathering, crane operating and snowmobile doctoring.

In Irwin, Biro learned the competence and self-reliance that has fed his status as a semi-legend. "You have to be your own plumber, electrician and mechanic here," he said. "If your snowmobile breaks, you fix it or you walk. You can't call a taxi or a tow truck. And try getting a plumber here in January."

Though Biro enjoys the summer social scene, when Irwin bustles with lake parties, homeowner association meetings and town picnics, he waxes poetic about the spell cast by the Irwin winters.

"Living here is magical," he said. "People get up here and they're stunned, in awe; they don't want to leave. People get downright sappy."

Biro said that, besides the "helmet head" caused by the snowmobile commute, the hardest thing about living at Irwin is leaving. The best thing: "Sunrise out on the deck with a cup of coffee, fighting off Stellar's jays and gray jays. Quiet and peace and privacy. Access to the debauchery and culture of Crested Butte, then a chance to leave that behind, get back to Irwin and go, 'Ahhh…'."

Biro figures he's about due for a gold watch for his tenure at Irwin. "I'm regularly tempted to move to Costa Rica," he said. "We talk about it all the time, but we'll never do it. I'll be here for another hundred years or so. You might as well do the story about me. Just one thing, though: I want Clint Eastwood to play my character in the movie. Stallone and Cruise are too short."

▲   Sojourners near Kebler: "The journey is the destination." Photo: Demerson

▲ Alpine flotsam and jetsam on a Third Street shed. Photo: Demerson

▶▶ Amid rust and splinters, nature continually renews herself. Photo: Runge

Stories written in wood

History gets downright personal in Crested Butte.

As with most things, Crested Butte does history a little differently.

I traveled recently to Europe and stood awed beneath magnificent structures, some a thousand years old, where the Roman Empire collapsed, DaVinci changed the course of art and Hitler prompted a world-wide war.

Then I came home to Crested Butte, where we advertise our National Historic District.

Well, yes, some history did happen here. The Jokerville Mine explosion killed 59 men in 1884. Butch Cassidy occasionally holed up in some bluffs out Cement Creek and hit Crested Butte for supplies and refreshment (though Jake Kochevar says the outlaw never actually left his pistol behind at Kochevar's Bar as the popular story holds). Old World immigrants settled here to work the coal mines early in the twentieth century. Rupert Smith's foresighted Law Science Academy brought doctors and lawyers together to discuss issues in the semi-deserted town in the late 1950s, after most of the mines had closed. The ski area opened in 1961, with a borrowed, ear-assaulting generator because the electric company hadn't quite finished its installation. All interesting, but hardly of global importance, and by my recent European standards, downright embarrassing.

But yesterday I drove by 215 Sopris Avenue, the tiny purple house with pink window boxes that was my home for 15 of its 120 years. I always smile when I drive past. There many years ago my husband reverently uncoiled his first climbing rope, I opened the *Pilot* newspaper to celebrate my first local by-line and our infant son pronounced his first word: "bah" ("ball," portending future closet contents). Now *that's* significant history.

The Sopris house reminds me why Crested Butte's National Historic District has its place alongside the grand landmarks of Europe. Those mighty monuments are like epic history books that sweep across the centuries, while Crested Butte's old buildings are like intimate journals hand-written by good-hearted, hard-working, everyday people.

The Sopris house sits low and tiny, presumptuous only in its color scheme (let's pretend somebody else chose that purple). While we lived there, the house felt cold, cramped and crooked, but fairly sang of untold stories. The Stefanic family supposedly raised eight kids in those 850 square feet, with all the drama that surely entailed. In our turn we hosted our own dramas. There I watched the home pregnancy test stick turn baby-bootie blue, Mom called to tell me of the disease that would kill her, and my son Chris lost his first tooth in a crack between the wall and the floor (fortunately the Tooth Fairy came anyway).

The sheetrock hides my husband Michael's initials, carved on a beam during his construction of the loft. He found other mystery initials in the walls, scrawled by some of the former owners who patched together that home with more affection than expertise. To redo the flooring, we excavated through four layers of varied linoleum, the archeological strata of previous shoestring remodels. Sandwiched in between were Croatian newspapers from the 1930s, insulation ã la Crested Butte.

For 15 years I nurtured a love-hate relationship with that house. I don't care to go back to the coal dust sifting from the attic or the icicles hanging from the shower curtain. But those drafty old walls framed some of the most momentous times of my life, and I love them for it.

The Sopris house helps me understand Molly Minneman's view of Crested Butte. To her, the Butte's neighborhoods of small old houses are like long shelves of storybooks, each holding its own irreplaceable collection of tales. "Each building has its own set of dreams placed on it," she said. As preservation officer for the Town of Crested Butte, Molly has heard or read enough of those stories to feel for the whole town what I feel for the Sopris house.

▲ Third Street and Maroon Avenue: In the brief lull between snowfalls, Crested Butte's homeowners go crazy for color. Photo: Spahn

◄ Jan Runge's front-porch garden. Photo: Leacock

"Each year I fall in love with Crested Butte that much more as I learn more about its roots," she said. "When I first came here, I liked the old buildings and their characteristics. But today I see so much more behind them. It's like when you meet a group of people, like a boyfriend's family. At first you like some more than others. Then as you get to know their personal histories, you understand them better and they become more fascinating, individually and as a group."

For those of us who grew up in modern, cookie-cutter suburbs, Crested Butte's uncomplicated but unique old homes ("like we drew houses in preschool," Molly noted) seem odd but generally charming.

"Buildings are the vernacular of a people," she said. "Our super simple buildings tell a story of the working people. People were real here, not trying to be something they weren't. It's not that they weren't smart or ingenious. But they lived with what they had. They made their lives rich in ways besides money."

To Molly's eyes, Crested Butte's basic architectural lines embody the values of its oldtimers: honest, practical and unpretentious. Adornments stand out: the bell towers that crown the churches, rock school and Old Town Hall or decorative touches on otherwise plain homes. The close clustering of Crested Butte's historic homes stemmed from economic necessity, but also reflected the intimacy fostered in such a remote, interdependent community.

Molly's favorite structures aren't necessarily the stately, dolled-up Victorians. She likes the "well-loved" homes, like Grace Arnott's one-story bungalow at 409 Maroon Avenue. Often she is drawn to a grouping of homes and outbuildings and the way they relate to each other. She has found that most people have favorite blocks or neighborhoods in Crested Butte.

"It's not really the individual buildings; it's the collection. All together, this is one of the best preserved representations of a workingman's town."

Molly cites the 100 block of Maroon Avenue, a row of houses constructed a century ago by the mining company for its employees and their families, anchored by the Elk Mountain Lodge, built as a boardinghouse for the bachelor miners. Though the houses looked similar, only three had running water; those probably went to the more skilled laborers, Molly said. "There were socioeconomic differences even among the miners. But they all went to the outhouse."

Over time, these miners' houses, like most of Crested Butte's old homes, have been remodeled by a progression of owners. It reminds me of the progressive story game, where one person starts a yarn, which is then expanded and passed on

▲ At 125 years and counting, the Union Congregational Church has aged ever so gracefully. Photo: Demerson

to each new storyteller until the tale strays far from the creator's initial vision. Likewise, the builder of our old Sopris house might scarcely recognize it now.

In Crested Butte, the remodeling process is guided by the Board of Zoning and Architectural Review. BOZAR was born in the 1970s, when far-sighted planners like Myles Rademan led the charge to create a National Historic District and architectural review processes. The goal: to preserve the sense of stories past while accommodating the people moving in, with stories yet to be told.

"There's a certain spirit held in these buildings," Molly said. "That's what people subconsciously respond to when they drive through town."

Occasionally as I drive by the Sopris house at night, I try to peer in the living room window if the curtains are open. I don't know who lives there, and they don't know whose initials are carved on their beams. But I believe my stories are part of the "certain spirit" people feel when they walk past that purple cottage. I'm glad I wrote my entries into its perpetual journal.

With that thought, I can echo Molly's wish: that we might value every Crested Butte house not because it changed the course of the world, but because it might have some former little resident's baby tooth lost in its cracks.

▲   Elk Avenue, looking east: New buildings have joined ranks with old ones; can you tell the difference? Photo: Leacock

▲◀◀ An old homestead and its outbuildings, settling imperceptibly back into the landscape. Photo: Leacock

◀   An elegant and pampered Elk Avenue doll house. Photo: Bilow

◀◀   Character wrought by weather. Photo: Leacock

▲ Christine Button and Nancy Jones joy-riding in the snow. Photo: Leacock

▶▶ Ellie Deacon (far right) and her fellow Butte Beauties take a mid-hike rest and chat at the summit of Mt. Crested Butte.

Rich beyond money

The hair-raising adventures of Ellie Deacon and her buddies.

Before Ellie Deacon discovered Crested Butte, she knew just how much to tip the room service personnel at the Ritz-Carlton, but she had not yet learned to savor a smashed peanut butter and jelly sandwich washed down with a swig of warm Gatorade.

Ellie had no idea that Crested Butte would change her life, perhaps even save it, when she first visited the town for her husband's 1984 meeting of the St. Petersburg Trial Lawyers Association. Sure, learning to ski at age 44 was a hoot, prompting her to buy ski boots, then skis, then shop for a condo so she wouldn't have to lug all that stuff around. After touring many resorts, the Deacons returned to the "darling little town" of Crested Butte to buy their ski condominium. The condo, before they remodeled, was a mess, but Crested Butte turned into an unexpected treasure.

Crested Butte came to Ellie's rescue in 1989, when she was 48, newly retired and stuck in an emotional pit. "I was terribly depressed," she said. "I probably wouldn't be here today without Crested Butte; that's how depressed I was."

After Ellie settled into the Butte for a summer-long stay, her condo manager invited her to play bridge with a group of women who mentioned they also hiked together. Though Ellie's primary hiking experience was the mall corridor between Saks and Neiman-Marcus, they invited her along.

Thus Ellie joined the Butte Beauties, then an informal group of a dozen women over age forty — now an organized group of more than a hundred women over age fifty. The women gather for weekly outdoor adventures and occasional trips and parties.

"Each summer I've learned something new," Ellie said. "Backpacking, whitewater, hiking up mountains. That first summer I got the 'Rookie of the Year' award because I was willing to do anything."

Ellie badly wanted to "fit in with the girls" but found herself in "high falutin'" company, with women like Martha Walton, Ann Clark and Jean Gardiner. "These women do things like climbing mountains and riding their bikes across the U.S."

Ellie's prim and proper background offered little help. Raised in Washington, D.C., she attended an exclusive all-girls convent for twelve years, learning to curtsy to royalty, serve tea and wear white gloves without soiling them. Her main tools for facing the great outdoors were humor and stubbornness.

"Everyone had to put up with me," she said of her new Crested Butte friends. "They did a lot of encouraging."

After her first three-month stay in Crested Butte, Ellie headed home to Florida. "My husband said, 'You are a different person.' I found nature, I found friends, I found exercise. Crested Butte renewed me. It was magnificent. I've never been depressed since."

Among the outdoor skills she learned in Crested Butte, Ellie eventually tackled an all-important one: pottying without a powder room. She had managed to "hold it" for a number of hikes, but P-Day loomed with an overnight horseback excursion planned by the original Butte Beauty, Phila Weatherly. Ellie prepared by taking horseback riding lessons, but there were no lessons for that other little challenge.

The first few miles of the trip were beautiful, but Ellie's saddle slowly slipped sideways until she found herself torqued and in tears. Once that was remedied, the ladies rode uneventfully to their scenic campsite beneath the Castles, but a friend observed that Ellie still seemed disgruntled. When Ellie admitted, "I haven't been to the bathroom all day," their guide disappeared for a few minutes. When he returned, he said, "I've dug you a hole, put a seat over it, wrapped a canvas curtain around it and left a roll of toilet paper in there for you. Now get in there and go to the bathroom." It was the first time since Ellie was a toddler that she received applause for that particular activity.

Ellie redeemed herself by catching three fish for the ladies' breakfast, then

▲ Another fly-fishing convert: The fish nibbled the fly and Amy Smithers caught the bug. Photo: Stillo

got in trouble for breaking a trip rule by bringing her makeup.

With characteristic gumption, Ellie has stuck it out through many a Butte Beauty adventure that stretched her comfort zone beyond recognition. On one hike, the women had to detour around a steep snowfield, requiring a climb up a treacherous slope. Ellie kept thinking, "It'll take them three to four years to find my body." Still, she persevered, once again to the cheers of her buddies.

Ellie's Crested Butte friends heap on the encouragement, but seldom miss a chance to tease. Luckily, Ellie loves to laugh at herself as well. She readily admits to her "vanity" about her teased blond hair, which has earned her the nickname "Q-tip."

"I'm the only one who never gets her hair wet," Ellie said. When a rainstorm drenched the Beauties on their hike to Aspen, Ellie whipped on a shower cap in the middle of the wilderness. "I had a perfect hairdo for Aspen; everyone else was a mess," she said. When the group went rafting, she deftly avoided moisture while all other raft occupants got soaked. When they learned to paddle inflatable ducky kayaks, Ellie sneaked her trusty shower cap on before donning her helmet.

For years, Ellie spent four months in Crested Butte each summer and three months each winter (turning into a "pretty good skier" thanks to her persistence and Kim Reichhelm's ego-boosting Women's Ski Adventures). Her extended stays allowed her to volunteer for several causes, like the Wildflower Festival, Reel Fest and Chamber Music Festival. "I gave myself to the community, and it gave a whole new meaning to my life," she said.

Lately her time in the Butte has shrunk as her kids and grandkids clamor for her babysitting services. But after each stay in Crested Butte, Ellie still returns to Florida refreshed and full of stories to tell her wide-eyed friends back home. "They're always interested to find out what I did. I'm the only one who has stories to tell."

Returning to her affluent Florida circles also reminds Ellie how unique and special her Crested Butte friendships are.

"When we get together it doesn't make any difference whether you have a $3 million home or a $75,000 condo, wear beautiful jewelry or no jewelry, wear a lot of makeup or none. It's a group of women from different states and avenues of life who get together and have fun. There's no criticism, cliques or talking behind backs, just wonderful, supportive friends. You don't have to impress anyone; we're all even. That's the most important thing I've learned."

▲ Settled into his hunting camp for the night, Christian Robertson conjures images of elk herds. Photo: Stillo

◄ Margaret Schaffer goes for the green on Trail 401. Photo: Stillo

◄◄ Robyn and John Norton escape the summer bustle by cruising the Taylor River (their youngest daughter's namesake). Photo: Stillo

151

▲ Mt. Crested Butte unfurls a welcome banner of snow. Photo: Demerson

▲▶ Fireworks at dusk, with mountains in silhouette. Photo: Bilow

▼▶ Mood lighting, compliments of alpine twilight. Photo: Bilow

▼ A rare aurora borealis halo wraps its eerie shine around Mt. Crested Butte. Photo: Demerson

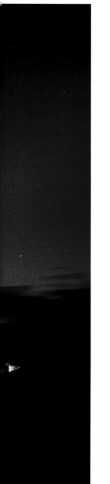

▲ On gentle summer nights, friends gather around the fire at Genevieve Bachman's house above Elk Avenue.

Family
by
Place

&

Beyond our
differences,
we create
a community
of place

Chris Ladoulis

▲ Crested Butte's current version of the trusty steed, outside the Idle Spur on Elk Avenue. Photo: Demerson

▶▶ Carol Garcia encircled by grandkids. Photo: Stillo

Connected by heartstrings

After years of giving, the Garcia family learned to receive.

Carol Garcia has a large family in Crested Butte: fifteen family members by blood (four kids and eleven grandkids); a handful by marriage; and a thousand or so by heartstrings. "I feel like the whole town is my family," she said. "I still get teary-eyed when I think about what this community has given me."

A self-proclaimed "city girl" from southern California, Carol surprised her husband Gary by adapting readily to life with their four kids in the tiny, dirt-street town of Crested Butte back in 1972. When Gary retired from piloting jets fifteen years later and built the Idle Spur restaurant/brewery on Elk Avenue, she adapted again; she worked in the background while Gary made his jovial rounds, shaking hands, hollering across the restaurant to greet customers by name, and generally sharing his joyful appetite for life. Like her kids, who also helped with the restaurant, she sighed with affectionate exasperation as Gary gave away untold amounts of food, drinks and use of the restaurant to raise money for groups or individuals in need. "Gary gave and gave and gave," Carol recalled. She had no idea that she and Gary would soon learn to receive as well.

At the end of a hectic Arts Fair weekend in 1995, Gary hopped on his motorcycle to deliver a tap for a keg party up at Irwin. Carol finished her work at the restaurant, ate dinner with visiting relatives and waited for Gary to join them. And waited. She heard sirens and grew increasingly uneasy. Finally she headed home, dashed for the ringing phone and picked up the receiver to hear the words she'd feared: "Carol, there's been an accident…".

On his return ride from Irwin, Gary hadn't been going particularly fast, according to the tourists driving down the dirt road behind him. Maybe he was scanning the hillsides for deer and elk, as he often did. Perhaps that's why he didn't see the culvert that sent him cartwheeling slowly over the front of his bike.

EMTs responded quickly to the 911 call and found a man torn up beyond recognition; they had no idea until later that they were scrambling to save the life of a friend. Gary was helicoptered by Flight for Life to St. Mary's Hospital in Grand Junction, where Carol and the rest of the family were summoned.

A high spinal injury left Gary paralyzed from the neck down, and life as they'd known it screeched to a halt. Gary, with Carol almost constantly by his side, hovered in intensive care for more than a month, then moved to Craig Hospital in Denver. There he faced several months of rehabilitation, learning how to live inside a body he could no longer move or control.

Meanwhile, the community of Crested Butte was doing what it does best: forming ranks behind a friend in need. Bonnie McNaughton loaned the Garcias $50,000 as a deposit for Craig Hospital when their insurance company balked. A local lawyer they'd never met volunteered to deal with the insurance company. Cards, calls, flowers and plants poured into Gary's hospital room, along with reports of how people had jumped in to help back at home.

In Crested Butte, a community-wide fundraising campaign drew involvement from people the Garcias had befriended or helped and from people they had never met. Businesses donated auction items, hairdressers hosted a cut-a-thon, second homeowners sent checks and an impromptu committee organized a dinner fundraiser. The Garcia boys and buddies built a new room and installed an elevator at their parents' Crested Butte home. Friend Gil Gillespie shaved his head to raise $10,000 in donations, followed by the Garcias' son Randy. "They looked so silly. But they did whatever it took," Carol said. "The community raised an incredible $90,000."

Trapped in their hospital room, Carol and Gary watched through tears of gratitude when friends sent a video of the events, filled with loving messages from the people who had jammed the restaurant on their behalf.

"It was unbelievable," Carol recalled. "The gifts kept coming, big and small. It was like the whole town said, 'We're here for you.' We felt so cushioned by this outpouring of love."

When the Garcias returned home, friends came daily to visit, move Gary and assist with his therapy.

▲ Warmly welcomed in 2005, Crested Butte Mountain Resort owners Tim and Diane Mueller (center) catch the first ride of the season with son Ethan, the resort's director of operations, and ski school director Charlie Farnan. Photo: Gallaher

■ Jim Harlan, world hand-cycling champ and Paralympics contender. Photo: Stillo

▼ Three generations: Alan and Marcia Hegeman with their daugher, son-in-law and grandbaby, Laura, Robert and Lillian Brodie. Photo: Bilow

"That helped Gary's spirits a lot. It showed him how much he was loved," Carol said.

Gary could no longer use his body, but he still had strength of will and the gift of gab. "He was the strong one for all of us," Carol said. With his speaker phone and voice-activated computer, Gary eased back into community involvement. As a board member for the Adaptive Sports Center, he helped organize the Red Lady Open, rousted volunteers and collected donations. With Carol or his assistant, Arturo, he sometimes rode his wheelchair downtown to visit friends. He seemed stronger, and Carol held hope that he would make progress against the paralysis.

But after some cysts were removed from his spine, Gary's condition began to deteriorate. "What little he felt was pain," Carol said. He began to spend more time at home, getting the household organized. "It was like he knew and was getting everything ready."

In August of 2001, six years after his accident, a cough quickly progressed to pneumonia, until even dramatic efforts couldn't save Gary's life. Once again, the community closed ranks to support Carol and her family.

Within a few years, Carol developed rheumatoid arthritis, underwent surgery to remove a brain tumor, and lost her husband, both parents and a brother. Then an "honorary son," Tommy Villanueva, died in an accident just south of Crested Butte. Tommy was her son Joe's best friend, and the son of her own childhood friend, Jennie. His death prompted another wave of compassion from the community and gave Carol a chance to pass on to the Villanueva family some of the kindness she had received.

"When such a catastrophic accident happens to someone you know, you do whatever you can. It helps ease the pain of watching what they have to go through."

Through her adversities, Carol has grown appreciative rather than bitter. "It makes you want to live your whole life like it might end tomorrow. That's what these things have taught us. Enjoy every day, love each other, love where we live. Enjoy this wonderful world we're blessed enough to be in."

In 2005, Carol sold her home, earned her real estate license and made plans to travel. "But I always want to come home to Crested Butte," she said. "I've been through a lot here. But I'm so lucky. I have all four of my kids here, almost all of my grandkids, and a whole community of people I could call on in an instant. How many women can live in a place for 32 years and still be in love with it?"

▲ Memorial Day draws returning oldtimers and local veterans together for the parade down Elk Avenue to the cemetery. Photo: Bilow

■ Willard and Ronnie Ruggera host family and friends who come "home" for Crested Butte's Memorial Day reunion. Photo: Bilow

◄ Ben Somrak and Chandra Nellis looking dapper for the Crested Butte Mountain Heritage Museum's Black and White Ball. Photo: Bilow

◄◄ These newlyweds launched their honeymoon, intentionally or not, by joining the July Fourth parade. Photo: Spahn

▲   Paradise Divide looms large behind a solitary Nordic skier east of Crested Butte. Photo: Bilow

▶▶   Native son Andrew Kastning couldn't wait to leave Crested Butte, and then to come back. Photo: Demerson

Coming home

How Andrew Kastning learned to appreciate that whole "it takes a village" thing.

When four-year-old Andrew Kastning climbed to the summit of Teocalli Mountain, after hiking through grass taller than he was, he gazed out over the expanse below and thought, "My valley." Fourteen years later, in 1999, Andrew's valley felt smaller than his grade-school sneakers; his parents blinked back tears as he boarded the plane bound for the University of Vermont, but he was "tugging at the leash to get out of there."

Now Andrew is back, with fresh eyes and a passel of friends. "They say, 'I can't believe you grew up here. This place is so special.' Stuff I've taken for granted, they're bloodthirsty to see and do," he said.

Looking through his friends' eyes, Andrew sees the preciousness of his Crested Butte childhood. He grew up outdoors: scrambling with his father Bill on "Rocky Hill," the scree field that served as a jungle gym behind his home in Crested Butte South, exploring four-wheel-drive roads in the family's VW bus, skiing at the resort and on Nordic trails, playing baseball, hiking and climbing mountains. During his high school years, he tried to summit two fourteeners (peaks over 14,000 feet elevation) per summer.

The town of Crested Butte was Andrew's childhood kingdom; he and his friends explored with an independence unknown to city kids. The community looked after him; when he skinned his knee playing in town, his mother Carol, a teacher-counselor at the elementary school, received half a dozen calls within a few minutes from people who had seen him crying while riding his bike down the street. Life was stable and consistent; "moving from one bedroom to another was the biggest deal," he said.

As he grew, the comfort of the small town became more confining. "I was pegged as extremely competitive, a good kid whose mother you had to answer to if you got in trouble at school," he said. "I felt locked into something that wasn't me. I was itching to meet new people so I could set up shop all over and be the person I really was. Crested Butte had become claustrophobic, emotionally and personality-wise."

After leaving his tearful parents at the airport, Andrew settled into the University of Vermont at Burlington. The city was as different as he'd hoped; it made Crested Butte seem like a bubble, removed from issues that plagued the rest of the world. The terrorist attacks of September 11, 2002, hit during his sophomore year. "Kids were crying, people were running around, fighter planes were thundering overhead on patrol from Green Mountain Air Force Base. Crested Butte seemed so far away."

Andrew carried with him the benefits of growing up in the Butte. He found that he was more self-directed and confident than most of his city-bred classmates getting their first taste of independence. He wasn't shy, because he grew up in a town where he knew almost everyone. He and other small-town kids became natural recreation directors among their peers. "The majority of kids out there, especially from cities, look for something to make their fun for them. Kids from small towns know how to make fun for themselves. We'd go sea kayaking, form a softball team, create a relay race.... We knew how to make fun, because we'd always done it."

Andrew also took from Crested Butte a life-long interest in the outdoors and in Nordic skiing. He studied wildlife biology and skied for Vermont's Nordic team — successfully, even though he outgrew his younger competitiveness as he became more comfortable with himself.

"I got more laid-back in college. I made friends, stopped talking about the latest ski race, and smiled a heck of a lot more," he said.

As anxious as he'd been to leave Crested Butte, Andrew took only three months to gain a little perspective on his hometown. "When I came home for Christmas my freshman year and drove around that corner at Round Mountain,

▲ A good-night kiss from the sun: the evening view from Skyland of Crested Butte and Paradise Divide. Photo: Bilow

◀ The Dyke formation near Kebler, framed by autumn hues. Photo: Leacock

I realized this place was pretty cool," he said. "I'd been more focused on getting out than on what I was leaving behind."

By his senior year in college, Andrew felt eager to spend time with his family again, and to share his hometown with close friends from Vermont. When seven college buddies visited Crested Butte for the Kastnings' graduation celebration, Andrew convinced six of them to join him living in the Butte the following winter.

"My mom said we were a Crested Butte version of 'Friends,'" he said.

His companions were enthralled by Crested Butte. "The first thing people noticed was the beauty: a small town surrounded by a big amphitheater of beautiful mountains. Then they noticed the people, the characters. Then they saw how fun it is here. My friends were pretty blown away by the Alley Loop [Nordic ski race]…the costumes, the big-air jump on the main street. People here know how to have fun."

A little uncertain how it would feel to move back, Andrew protected his anonymity with a beard for a while. Now the beard is gone and he even enjoys the occasional, "I knew you back when…."

Several of Andrew's former high school classmates have also moved back to Crested Butte, including Hunter Dale, Max Mancini, Royal White, Tommy Rozman and Brian Kray. Andrew said the trend might be partly for economic reasons, but also because "we're starting to recognize how unique our youth was here."

A few years' distance has allowed Andrew to more fully appreciate some of those old friendships. "I've known Hunter almost all my life; he was born nine days before me. Max and I learned to ski together. Now that I look back at it, I see the value of knowing someone my whole life."

Still weighing options for his future, Andrew is considering graduate school in environmental planning, perhaps studying wildlife population issues such as how genetics are affected as elk herd territories become smaller and more fragmented. "I'll always need a job that gets me outside," he said. Eventually he might settle in Crested Butte, with the caveat that he travels often to remember the worlds beyond "his valley."

"This would be a great place to raise my kids," Andrew said, laughing at his eagerness to leave a few years ago. "It took me a while to appreciate the whole 'it takes a village to raise a child' thing."

▲ Pint-sized pumpkins and princesses ponder this whole strange Halloween thing. Photo: Bilow

▼ Tassels fly as the Crested Butte Community School Class of 2005 bids adieu to its alma mater. Photo: Ladoulis

▲ Summit Hike participants trek each August to honor cancer victims and support the Living Journeys support group. Photo: Bilow

▲ Hang-gliders take flight from Crested Butte Mountain to soar over the valley floor. Photo: Bilow

▲ The Hellands, Vosburgs and Garrens, extended family... extended beyond bloodlines. Photo: Ladoulis

▶▶ Earth, air, sky: elemental art. Photo: Spahn.

Saying grace

By MJ Vosburg

The setting looks like many homes on Thanksgiving Day. Three tables have been linked together to form one long family table. My mother's tablecloth is ironed and spread. The rarely used china from my grandmother, JuJu, is proudly displayed. Generations of recipes have been consulted and tweaked (how did Mom get such perfect gravy every time?). It's time to eat.

We call everyone to the table. This isn't the usual assortment of grandparents, aunts, uncles and cousins. I look at the people who have become my family and am overwhelmed with emotion. Gathered around me are the people I've come to love and depend on every day. I realize the last twenty-four years in Crested Butte have given me a circle of friends that offers the best of what "family" means.

This Thanksgiving feast brings our friends the Hellands and Fails/Garrens to the table. The meal reflects a true group effort. There are borrowed chairs and serving pieces, food from many heritages and each family's special dessert requests.

The Vosburg family is not overly religious, so the Thanksgiving blessing does not flow gracefully. We are unaccustomed to expressing our thankfulness in a formal manner. When I suggest that we go around the table and say what we are grateful for, six sets of teenage eyes roll back in shaking heads. I volunteer to go first.

"I'm grateful we live in Crested Butte."

Unlike many residents of the Butte, I do not live here for the vast recreational opportunities. I don't mountain bike, ski the extremes, kayak or golf. I'm good for a hike (with friends), a cross-country ski and maybe a little tennis. What has kept me in Crested Butte is my relationships. I've made the best friends possible here. And the wide spectrum of relationships amazes me every day. People seem to care more about each other here. They feel a sense of safety and trust. Okay, the town has grown a lot since I moved here. I take some responsibility for that; it was my generation that said, "Hey, we're not leaving just because we're getting older and want to have a family and real jobs." And while more aspects mimic the city-life we avoid, the values of the community remain true. If you have to have a crisis in your life, have it in Crested Butte. You'll get incredible support.

"I'm grateful for my girlfriends."

Two of the best, Sandy and Connie, are sitting at the table. It seems very "in" to talk about the relationships between women these days, but I had girlfriends before girlfriends were cool. They are such an integral part of my life that I can hardly imagine life without them. I've had good friends throughout my life, but in Crested Butte I feel a different level of trust and comfort. Perhaps the vast wilderness surrounding our cozy town prompts me to take more risks in my relationships. My girlfriends have raised me up during tough times and settled me down during crazy times. They love me in spite of flaws and mistakes.

My kids, Emma and Zach, think of Sandy and Connie as aunts. Emma was a mama's girl until she was about eight, so the transition from home to school sometimes involved drying her tears and prying her death grip from my leg. Then Connie (the school office manager) would show up. "How are you doing today, Miss Em?" That was enough. In third grade, Emma honored their relationship with an inscription in a book of poetry she wrote: "To my good friend Connie."

"I'm grateful to be in love."

Crested Butte makes a wonderful place to be in love. Joel and I launched our romance in college, but we've spent our entire married life in Crested Butte. In the early days, the exciting and adventurous aspects of life here fed our passion for each other. Crested Butte was just one big block party. As our marriage evolved, our reasons for staying in CB changed. It was the ideal place to raise our children. We've been able to find careers that complement the lifestyle we want. We've probably taken bigger risks here than we would have in a more urban place. Crested Butte also offers endless opportunities to get involved and contribute to the community, which we've enjoyed over the years. At times Joel (Mr. Booster Club) has put more time and energy into removing snow from the school's track than into planning our

▲ Bearing friendships almost as long as their old-time wooden skis: parade regulars Don Mancini, Brian Dale, Marilyn Mancini, Jim Gebhart and Bill Kastning. Photo: Runge

◄ Local biking sweeties Xavi Fane and Karen Janssen. Photo: Bilow

anniversary. I might not always applaud that, but I recognize that volunteering feeds our souls and makes us better spouses for each other. As our hair grays and joints stiffen, we talk about winters in a warmer place. One day we probably will head south for part of each year, but our hearts belong to Crested Butte and it will always be a part of us.

"I'm grateful Zach, Chris and Peter have been raised like cousins."

We live far from our "real" relatives, so my kids get few opportunities to visit their cousins. But Zach, Chris and Peter have spent countless days together since birth. Besides learning to talk and walk together, they learned to camp, ski, play soccer, meet girls, play poker and probably a few things I won't know about for a long time. The three returned from a trip to Spain with three freshly pierced ears. They've gotten in trouble together and celebrated successes together. Because Chris and Peter are a few months older than Zach, they will head to college while Zach does his senior year of high school. As Zach so eloquently put it, "It's gonna suck." But I'm not too worried; these boys have a bond that will last a lifetime.

"I'm grateful for vacations."

I grew up in a large family with limited resources; we never took vacations. I'm making up for lost time. Getting out of our home environment reminds us to appreciate it even more. We often travel with our Crested Butte family, generally to places involving warmth, sand and coral reefs. The Vosburgs, Hellands, Chlipalas and Fails/Garrens have learned to love the ocean together, and our memories (on land and underwater) will last until Alzheimers sets in.

But traditions at home, like this Thanksgiving dinner, give me the peace I thrive on. Day-to-day life in Crested Butte — what could be better?

"I could go on and on about being grateful, but I'll stop with that. Anyone else?"

I'm so pleased when Peter volunteers to go next.

"I'm grateful MJ has finally finished so we can eat."

So much for the heartfelt gratitude of the moment. It's okay, though, because Connie and Sandy shoot me appreciative looks, another tradition shared with loved ones. Did I mention I'm truly thankful for that?

▲ The sign says it all. Photo: Demerson

◄ Good friends, plenty of trail mix and killer views. Photo: Stillo

▲ The East River, half frozen, still flowing. Photo: Demerson

▲ September snow nudges in on autumn's splendor. Photo: Leacock

▲ Winter residents: Early-winter passersby can almost always watch bald eagles soaring or posing in cottonwood branches above the East River north of Almont. Photo: Spahn

▶ Summer residents: Thousands of hummingbirds make their annual warm-weather pilgrimage to Crested Butte. Photo: Runge

▶▶ Long Lake: a scenic spot for repose or a bracing afternoon swim. Photo: Stillo

▲◀ Like many seasonal residents, after leaving for a few months, winter can't wait to get back to Crested Butte. Photo: Runge

▲▶ Alpine shooting star. Photo: Runge

◀ Autumn gold and winter white on a three-dimensional charcoal sketch. Photo: Runge

Photographers
& designer

Nathan Bilow

Through photography, Nathan has traveled the world. As official photographer for Kodak and the U.S. Ski Association, he documented two decades of Olympics. An Associated Press stringer and freelancer, he has hundreds of international credits, earning awards from the North American Ski Journalists and Colorado Ski Country. In the '80s he helped bring adventure racing to America through his photography. Nathan published two books, **The Edge of Paradise** and **The Seasons of Paradise**, and co-owns Rocky Mountain Impressions postcards. He enjoys telemarking, snowboarding, hiking, mountain biking, fly fishing and sharing Crested Butte with his wife and two children.

www.nathanbilow
photography.com

Dusty Demerson

Dusty has felt compelled to photograph since high school, to find and share unique viewpoints or encounters. His moment-in-time images come sometimes through waiting and watching, and sometimes as "gifts from the Creator." Dusty earned a journalism BA and an MBA and operated a photo lab/studio before deciding to photograph full time. Recently he has been featured in several exhibitions, winning awards in the Western Heritage Invitational, Hasselblad Super Circuit and Banff Mountain Film Festival. The Rijks Family Gallery features his work. Dusty lives in Mt. Crested Butte, where he heads the town's planning commission.

www.color-west.com

Paul Gallaher

Paul studied at the University of Texas, earning a B.S. in communications from the university that flunked Walter Cronkite. One day in 1981, he left the family cabin in Buena Vista bound for employment with a respected Aspen photo business, with a small detour to visit friends in Crested Butte. After a chance meeting with editor Lee Ervin, he ended the day as staff photographer for the *Crested Butte Pilot*, having gleefully accepted a big cut in pay. Paul has since worked for *National Geographic, Outside, Newsweek*, the major snow sports magazines and corporate clients, photographing everything from architecture to zebras. His motto: "Keep a beginner's mind; experts learn nothing."

www.visitcrestedbutte.com
/gallaher

Chris Ladoulis

Chris Ladoulis found himself in Crested Butte in 1999, having spent most of his life in Texas pursuing careers more lucrative but less satisfying than photography. Like many, he came to Crested Butte to learn how to focus on life instead of work. Living in a small community of happy people, filled with folks doing what they love, inspired Chris to pick up his camera and start shooting. He enjoys photographing people, often candid, seldom posed and usually smiling. His shots are catching attention from local media for their fun and spontaneity. Chris and his wife Kate live in town with their dog Django.

www.ladoulis.com

Jessy Moreland
Crested Butte Printing

Born in upstate New York, Jessy was labeled an artist almost from toddlerhood. A natural with many media, she attended Western State College in Gunnison for an education in art and mountain living. There she discovered graphic design, thinking outside the box to create art with a mouse and monitor instead of paintbrush or clay. After moves to Whistler, Denver and Lake Tahoe, Jessy hurried back to the healthier, more authentic, less materialistic lifestyle of the Gunnison Valley. She balances graphic design at Crested Butte Printing with oil painting and being outdoors with her sweetie, Joel Karinen, trail running, backcountry skiing and mountain biking.

J.C. Leacock

Since launching his career in 1988, J.C. has emerged as one of the premier photographers of the American West. His landscapes capture the light, grandeur and intimacy of the West, while his portrayals of western lifestyles are both authentic and spirited. J.C. is widely published locally and in national publications such as *Backpacker* and *Cowboys & Indians*. J.C. and his wife Kriste moved to Crested Butte in 2003. "The scenery, community and recreation make this an inspirational place to live and photograph," he said. J.C. loves to ski, mountain bike and horseback ride in the mountains around Crested Butte.

www.jcleacock.com

Jan Runge

In the late 1980s, Jan picked up a friend's camera and photographed him fishing. A few weeks later a hefty check arrived from *Sports Afield*, purchasing the photo for enough money that Jan could buy her own camera gear. A career was born. For Jan, a Colorado native who studied art at Western State College, photography brought together her intuitive knack for composition, hyperawareness of light and propensity to wander the backcountry with her horse and dog for long stretches of time. Jan's rich photos — flowers, landscapes and portraits — have graced Wildflower Festival posters, calendars and magazines.

email: rogirunge@msn.com

James Ray Spahn

James Ray Spahn chose Crested Butte as his home base because of the solitude, beauty and close community it offers him, his wife and their two children, but his reputation as a photographer extends far beyond the valley. An honor graduate of the Brooks Institute of Photography and Science in Santa Barbara, James has become a noted advertising and location photographer, with national and international clients. With his detailed, original and artistic eye, he contributes frequently to some of the top home publications in the country. He was one of only 50 photographers chosen for Hasselblad's 50th anniversary show, and his many magazine credits include *Architectural Digest*, *Country Home* and *Cowboys & Indians*.

www.jamesrayspahn.com

Tom Stillo

Tom loves his camera, but lives for his volleyball. In 2005, he played with the Quicksilver Legends alongside several former Olympians, winning the U.S. Open and World Masters. An all-around athlete, Tom loves the variety that photography brings him, from skiing with pros to capturing a wedding's tender moments. Winner of the Harold Hirsch Award for Snowsports Photography, Tom's images have appeared in countless national and international publications, from *National Geographic* to the *Wall Street Journal*, plus collateral for Chaco Sandals USA, Patagonia and other clients. His team includes his wife Jenny, son Justin and daughter/volleyball protégé Asya.

www.tomstillophoto.com

MJ, Emma, Joel and Zach Vosburg, Sandy Fails, Chris and Michael Garren at Crested Butte High School graduation 2005. Photo: Ladoulis

Sandy Fails

Sandy has been writing about Crested Butte and her mortified family members since moving here in 1981 with her new love Michael Garren and honors/journalism degree from the University of Texas. She has written for local newspapers, regional magazines and national publications; authored two previous books (**Crested Butte: The Edge of Paradise** and **The Seasons of Paradise**); and edited the *Crested Butte Magazine* for 19 years. In Crested Butte, Sandy also learned to ski, dress in layers, be a kid, raise a kid, drive on ice, shovel, volunteer, stop volunteering quite so much, and help run the family business, the Old Town Inn. Her best work to date is son Chris, co-produced with her husband Michael.

MJ Vosburg

MJ headed west from Nashville in 1976 and never looked back. After attending the University of Denver, she followed love to Crested Butte in 1981 to spend a year in the mountains. Twenty-four years, a wedding and two kids later, she's still here. Most of MJ's traditional jobs have involved marketing tourism within the valley. Her nontraditional jobs usually entail working for causes and committees on behalf of children and schools. To MJ, her friendships, volunteerism and heartfelt conversations define her life better than any professional resumé. Crested Butte has been the perfect setting for MJ, her husband, Joel, and their children, Zach and Emma, to pack their lives full of friends and adventures.

▲ Parry's primrose prefers waterfront property. Photo: Runge

▲ Standing its ground: Dusty Demerson titled this award-winning photo "Fearless."